Emotional Terrorism

BREAKING THE CHAINS
OF A TOXIC RELATIONSHIP

Emotional Terrorism

BREAKING THE CHAINS
OF A TOXIC RELATIONSHIP

Erin K. Leonard, L.C.S.W., Ph.D.

Green Dragon Publishing
P.O. Box 1608
Lake Worth, FL 33460

Emotional Terrorism : Breaking the Chains of a Toxic Relationship
A Green Dragon Publishing Group Publication

© 2014 Green Dragon Books
First Edition

Green Dragon Publishing
P.O. Box 1608
Lake Worth, FL 33460

Printed in the United States of America and the United Kingdom

ISBN (Paperback) 9781623860059

Library of Congress Cataloging-in-Publication Data Control # 2014937253

Acknowledgements

To my clients with heartfelt appreciation and gratitude;
this book would be nothing without your bravery, honesty,
and faith in humanity.

Thanks to the greatest joy in my life, my children,
for having an unwavering faith in their mom, and my parents
for their continuous and strong encouragement.

James Bayer, thank you for your open heart,
strong intelligence, and fresh ideas.

Tom Snelson, thank you for always making me laugh
when I want to cry!

A big thank you to the folks on "RCC" who love camaraderie
and Coors Delight on hot summer nights.

Thanks to Dr. Neil Spira, who started this crazy train
moving forward in the right direction.

Last but certainly not least, thank you to Ed Haley.

Finally I'd like to say thank you to Green Dragon Books
for sharing my vision in this project, and to my editor,
Ashley Cooper for tying it all together.

Introduction

What does it mean to be emotionally terrorized? Imagine living with a relationship that has you feeling like it would be easier if you were physically abused. Sometimes emotional and psychological abuse can leave painful wounds that feel far worse than physical. Dr. Erin Leonard, PhD., takes the reader on an in depth look into the world of "Projective Identification". Aiming to give a voice to the victims who suffer silently within the confines of this relationship dynamic, she explores a world of hurt, confusion and chaos. Many people have no idea they are in a relationship that is ruled by hate, they just know something is wrong and many times wonder, "Is this my fault?"

With the help of detailed case studies, stories of pain and survival are beautifully articulated through examples of the author's patients. The cases in this book are real, and you may find yourself relating to one or more of the stories shared. If you do, then perhaps you yourself, are a victim of projective identification. A form of abuse that often gets swept under the rug, because until now, it has not been widely understood. Through this book, you will learn the roles each person plays within projective identification. You will be introduced to the "projector", who actively seeks a person to infuse with their own intolerable characteristics, and the "recipient", whose good nature and desperation to be loved, leads them to the welcomed embodiment of their partner's negative traits. What comes next is a path of envy, turmoil and eventual destruction.

In modern days it has become routine to hear of tragic stories about children being bullied, who then take their own lives. What many people do not know is that bullying is a product of projective identification, and can occur not just in school children, but married couples, adults and in the work place. The concept of projective identification sheds light on how tragedies such as the Sandy Hook shooting, could possibly happen. As unthinkable tragedies unfold, we find traces of emotional terrorism intertwined within the fabric of the horrific events. The unstable relationship dynamic that leads people to dangerous acts, also finds a way to turn once happy marriages into divorces. The power of projective identification is insurmountable, and as we learn in the following chapters, the only way to end this dynamic is to stop the projector.

As we are invited into the lives of women and men who have been involved in projective identification relationships, we not only learn of the struggles they endured, but also of the courage they found within themselves to get out. Whether a person is feeling bullied in the workplace or by a spouse, they may be the recipients of a projector who has handpicked them receive their venomous bite. The only way to win against this entangling battle is to truly understand what you are going up against, and to fight with wisdom.

Chapter 1

WHAT IS PROJECTIVE IDENTIFICATION?

Many of us are familiar with the Freudian concept, or at least the term "projection". Projection is a defense mechanism that involves taking one's unacceptable qualities or feelings and assigning them to other people. We are often times guilty of engaging in some sort of projective behavior at some point in our own life. For example; if a person fears someone does not like them, they may in tern decided they do not like that person. This provides "safety" for that person's ego, as they have made themselves the rejecter as opposed to being rejected. *Projective Identification* is an extension of projection that quietly finds it's into many relationships causing feelings of guilt, shame, rage and envy.

There is great importance in understanding the power of projective identification which has the ability to extend beyond the damage of personal relationships. With the core emotion of hate being found at the root of this unconscious behavior, if allowed to manifest without intervention, it can cause a great deal of dysfunction and damage. Such a thing is so powerful that it has been linked historically to genocides, and found at the root of racism, sexism and other culturally threatening stigmas. Now imagine the impact such a powerful, psychological tool, can have when used within a personal relationship. The results of such an emotional attack can be both confusing and devastating.

There are three elements that establish projective identification; the projector, the recipient, and the unconscious material that is being transferred from the projector to the recipient. Projective identification offers a way for the projector to be aggressive while playing the role of the victim. Once the projector discovers aspects himself that he is unable to accept, he then unconsciously looks for a recipient to project his undesirable qualities. This gives the projector a sense of relief as he has successfully released himself of his own insecurities, and is now able to see the recipient as the weaker element in the relationship. He then manifests his ego based upon false ideals of himself, while berating the recipient for embodying all the things he disliked about himself.

The second part of the projective identification dynamic is the recipient. This person becomes a vessel for the projector's hated parts of himself. A recipient often times has low self-esteem which makes them vulnerable to the projective identification dynamic. However, it is important to note that while the recipient does indeed suffer from low self-esteem, theirs is still not as compromised as the projector's. Recipients are also described as being people pleasers and in many cases, oversensitive.

The third element in projective identification is the toxic unconscious material that is passed from the projector to the recipient. This material inherently belongs to the projector, yet, is too shameful for him to accept about himself. The projector then unconsciously places their own distressing qualities onto the recipient, in attempt to salvage their ego from breaking down. Once they have placed their undesirable qualities onto another, they've successfully moved that person (the recipient) into a position where they are able to be condemned and controlled. As a lion catches their prey, the projector unconsciously senses and is drawn to the vulnerability of the recipient. Initially charming in order to ensnare the recipient, the projector begins to transfer his toxic material to the recipient who accepts it without knowing. The acceptance of this material creates feelings of insecurity for the recipient, and while the projector actively breaks the recipient down, they simultaneously build their own self-esteem up.

Projective Identification can be found in examples outside of adult romantic relationships and within relationships such as parent/child, work environments, friendships, and within the cases of the childhood bully. A bully on the playground often presents themself as big and powerful when they are bullying another child. The child who is being bullied often times feels afraid and weak. Yet, inside, it is the bully who actually feels deeply insecure. As found in some cases, when the child who is being victimized decides to standup for themselves, many times the bully backs down. This can be attributed to the fact that the bully is no longer finding success within that particular child as a recipient for their toxic material. They must then move on and search for someone else who embodies the attributes of a desirable recipient.

Unfortunately, there are far too many cases that do not end quite as positively as the aforementioned example. Many children who are bullied lack the skills to effectively make their bully loose interest in them. The following are just a handful of the devastating cases that have made headlines in the United States:

Jessica Logan (1990-2008) a high school senior from Ohio, took her own life after enduring several months of harassment and bullying. She was repeatedly called derogatory slurs such as "whore" following the distribution of a provocative picture she had send to her boyfriend while they were in a relationship. After the breakup, he sent the picture of Jessica to her classmates. Unable to withstand the bullying, she hung herself in her bedroom closet with a hanger.

Tyler Clementine (1992-2010) a freshmen at Rutgers University and budding violinist, jumped from the George Washington Bridge after being bullied. Two dorm mates had videotaped Tyler having intercourse with another man and then streamed the video on the internet. While only speculative, one may assume the reason the two men took such an interest into Tyler's personal life could be attributed to an insecurity of their own.

Sarah Lynn Butler (1997-2009) a 12 year old seventh grader from Hardy, Arkansas who took her own life after being bullied for months. The last message she saw before hanging herself was "You will be easily forgotten. You are a stupid little naïve girl who nobody will miss." Again, for a child to write such words of hatred to classmate, one may assume they were speaking from a dark place of insecurity that they then projected onto Sarah.

While this is just a handful of examples of the lethalness projective identification can have, studies have been done in Britain finding that at least half of the suicides amongst young people were related to bullying. Research gathered by ABC news shows that nearly 30% of students are either bullies or victims of bullying, and 160,000 children stay at home from school every day because they are bullied. Learning how to properly identify characteristics of projector behavior, as well as recipient behavior can help to lessen this epidemic. Children should be taught how to stand up for themselves so not to fall victim to a bully who is looking for a recipient. Similarly, and perhaps, more importantly, children must be taught how to deal with and accept their inner flaws in a healthy manner so that they themselves do not become projectors.

Recruiting additional people to tear down the recipient along with them is often times the goal of the bully/ projector. Another common tactic is distorting the truth about the recipient in order to humiliate and destroy the recipient's reputation. Building alliances to go against the recipient not only feeds the projector's ego, the destruction of the recipient becomes all the more righteous and necessary for the projector to continue. The bully finally finds themselves in a position of power, and deems their "cause" honorable because they have found strength in the numbers they have created.

Although childhood bullying is a clear example of projective identification, the dynamic becomes increasingly complicated in adult relationships. As with any relationship entwined in projective identification, it is the recipient that usually suffers most in these relationships. Often they have persistent feelings of inadequacy around the projector and find themselves stroking their ego in order to appease them. Their need to please their projector seemingly protects them from being degraded or demeaned, and often times they become passive while surrendering to the belief that they are incompetent. When this occurs, the recipient often makes more "mistakes" because they have lost their self-esteem and are less confident in their abilities. In turn, this perpetuates the dynamic because now, preforming at a diminished capacity, the recipient feels their projector's deeming comments must be true.

If this dynamic cycle is continues, the recipient can become increasingly insecure. Even the most competent and successful people may believe that they are "less than" and deserve to be treated as such. This allows the cycle to continue as they slip into a dependent and subservient role because they have fallen into the belief that they "need" the projector. Many times this example of dysfunction can lead to domestic violence within relationships. Highly successful people who have obtained PhDs, law degrees, medical degrees and so forth find themselves entrenched in this dynamic. In some cases it is not until the recipient tries to leave the relationship that things take a scary turn for the worse. The projector suffers from a tragic sense of loss as they have become so deeply dependent on their recipient to validate any embodiment of strength and psychological balance. Without that person, they begin to personify all of the qualities they originally hated about themselves. Desperate to maintain the cycle they created, the projector panics, and in some cases becomes completely unraveled.

The domestic violence case involving Lucy Mundia and her daughter Shirley illustrates the aforesaid in a tragic series of events:

Lucy had been involved with Edward Mwaura for several years and was trying to end the relationship. Their daughter Shirley was 7 years old at the time. Edward broke in to Lucy's house in South Bend, Indiana and attempted to stab her repeatedly. A neighbor heard Lucy screaming, "He's going to kill my baby!" Once the neighbor arrived at Lucy's door, she was badly wounded. The neighbor grabbed her and helped her out of the house. Then, he heard a little girl screaming. He went around to the side of the house where he heard the screaming, and looked inside a window where he saw Shirley. The 7 year old was sitting on the bed yelling and crying, "Daddy, daddy!" The 911 worker advised the neighbor to stay away from the house because police were on their way. The neighbor did as told, when he heard two pops. The next time he saw Shirley, she had been stabbed several times and died at the hands of her father.

This tragedy exemplifies the power of projective identification and the psychological instability a projector feels when they lose the recipient they had been using for strength. This mental instability combined with rage, can be a lethal and deadly combination if directed towards the recipient or an extension of her. If the projector can't destroy the recipient, they will attack the closest thing to that person. It is most likely that Shirley, like her mother, had become a recipient for Edward.

According to advocates and law enforcement officials, it is crucial that the victims of domestic violence find a way out. In 2005, The FBI found that 1,181 women and 329 men were killed by intimate partners, with these numbers steadily increasing. Domestic violence is on the extreme end of the spectrum when dealing with projective identification, however due to the nature of its seriousness and rising toll, it is an important aspect to consider when looking at this kind of dysfunction in any relationship.

Chapter 2

MARRIAGE AND FRIENDSHIPS

Projective Identification can coincide with violence depending on the situation and how it progresses within relationships. However, in some marriages and friendships violent projective identification can subtly make its way inside undetected, because actual *physical* violence is not present. Hate appears in the form of disgust from the projector towards the recipient. Often times it is conveyed in degrading and condescending statements to the recipient. Communication takes the form of demands and criticisms, rather than an equal dialogue. It is at this juncture, that taunting and teasing may transpire. What once seemed to have good nature and humorous undertones, now is filled with malicious and devaluing qualities. Complaints and backhanded comments are common, and are delivered from a superior position that inherently degrades the recipient.

In many cases the projector is threatened by the success of the recipient, it is because of this that these achievements are devalued. For example, a partner who has an accomplished spouse who is returning to work, may say to his spouse on their first day, "Oh you've got your big girl panties on to go to your big girl job." In addition to being threatened by the recipient's success, the projector is often times threatened by their spouse's outside relationships. These too, are subjected to intense scrutiny, and in many cases name calling ensues. Calling the recipient's friends "whores" or "losers" is a technique often used by the projector as they try to convince the recipient that they are too good for their friends. The recipient wants to feel valued instead of feeling degraded so they are vulnerable to agreeing. A projector may also take the opposite approach by attempting to connect with the recipient's friends in order to learn information about their partners. Inherently paranoid, the projector can maintain a sense of control over the recipient by obtaining information about them, then using it against them.

A lack of empathy also exemplifies a projector's disgust for the recipient. If the recipient becomes ill or injured, the projector often acts as if the ailment is their fault. Rather than offering support to their partner or friend, the projector treats the recipient as if they deserve to be hurt or sick. This type of blaming becomes a constant factor in the relationship. The projector finds ways to blame the recipient for everything wrong in their own life and within their relationship. This allows the projector to complain about the recipient to friends and acquaintances. Their objective being to align the people in their life with them, and furthering their ability to dominate the recipient.

Perhaps the most destructive techniques the projector utilizes in their treatment and interactions with the recipient, is in the presence of their children. Disrespecting the recipient with rude comments, nasty looks, and even ignoring the recipient's presence, conveys to the child that the recipient is a "less than" partner in the relationship, and that the projector is "the boss". This dynamic teaches the children to ignore and degrade the recipient, again, putting the recipient at a devalued position within the family. If the recipient stands up for themselves and refuses to be disrespected, an argument ensues. A predicament the recipient usually aims to avoid for the sake of the children. However, if the recipient does make the decision to fight back, the projector uses this as an opportunity to frame them as "crazy" or "out of control" in front of their children.

With any given opportunity, the projector will attack the recipient directly or indirectly. There is also a refusal to participate and attend anything that the recipient may be involved. For example, the projector often refuses to go to the recipient's office parties or athletic events, stating that he is too busy to go…translation, he is too important to go. Male projectors will often times make sexist or misogynistic comments at or around their female recipient. If the recipient is a runner, the projector will make degrading comments about other runners in their presence. Although both genders can be projectors and recipients, the easiest way for a male projector to degrade a female recipient, is though sex. Often times demanding intercourse as if it is their right, and as if the recipient owes it to them. Sexually degrading comments abound and are mostly malicious.

Elane, had been married to her husband for six years. In one counseling session, she expressed fear at the extreme nature of some of her husband's text messages. For example, one evening while she was visiting her parent's house, he sent her a text message that said; "I bet your dad and brother won't like me after I tell them how you suck my cock." After talking about the text message in session, Elane realized it was the combination of the sexual degradation and aggression that was sickening. On another occasion, Elane, who happened to be a doctor, accompanied her husband to a party hosted by a surgeon with whom he worked. She ran into a colleague of her own, along with his wife and was happy to see familiar faces. Her husband, who was annoyed that she had her own connections at the party, approached her from behind as she was talking with her friends and groped her breasts in front of them, then loudly described how he was going to have sex with her when they got home. Demoralized and humiliated, Elane felt she had no choice but to laugh it off as a joke.

Another client, Molly, was also involved with a projector. He often groped her and demanded sex even if they hadn't had a conversation in days. In the presence of their nine year old daughter he stated to Molly, "I always like to smell something before I eat it," then he glared at Molly and chuckled. On another occasion, Molly was planning on going to the bank to make a deposit so she could pay their bills. Her husband approached her immediately after she had gotten out of the shower and was still in a bath robe. He physically attempted to shove the money underneath her robe, between her breasts. Tearful about the interaction, Molly believes this was an attempt to objectify her through money and sex, as if she were a stripper or prostitute. Eventually she decided to file for a divorce and six months into the preceding, Molly received a text from her husband that stated, "I'll give you a hundred bucks to come over here and rub my "legs". "You'll need the money."

Objectification is at the root of degradation. Treating a person as an object without regard to their dignity is the definition social psychologists apply to the term objectification. In many instances, a projector will treat their partner as an object or a possession and most often a vehicle for their sexual satisfaction. They will complement the recipient on superficial qualities, such as how they look, but will refrain from complimenting them on qualities which give the recipient human character and dignity. For example, a projector might say, "I like your hair." Or, "You look hot", but they will not say, "You are an intelligent, compassionate person."

In addition to interpersonal relationships, projective identification can be a dynamic present in many friendships. Intelligent, charismatic and charming at first, projectors easily reel in a recipient who is unconsciously looking for someone to connect with. Recipients are easily flattered by the projector's attention and humor. They are sometimes grateful that another human being has taken an interest in them and willingly invest in the relationship. Yet, there exists an unconscious pact that both parties are making without realizing it. The projector is usually "the boss" and the recipient is usually "the employee". The friendship can progress as long as the recipient does what the projector asks, which is usually to align with them against another recipient in their repertoire. If the recipient refuses to participate in the other recipient's demise, the projector becomes silently enraged and attempts to align others against this recipient. It is, at its best, seventh grade mean girl behavior.

Afraid of being ostracized from the group, the recipient sometimes compiles to "save their own skin". This is equivalent to adult bullying, which is prevalent in American culture today. Adults model these tactics for their children without being consciously aware that they are doing so. Yet, when their child is bullied, they become infuriated at the unfairness of the situation, not realizing that they perpetuate it as well.

tionship, but transitions to devaluing them as the relationship is solidified. For example, in the case of Elane, her husband made statements in the onset of their relationship such as, "You're a doctor, those people work for you." Yet, as the relationship progressed, he would say, "I don't even know why you work, you don't make any money," and, "You work with crazy people because you know how they think." The projector will use idealization to reel the recipient into the relationship, then implement projective identification to keep them.

Due to their inability to regulate their moods and emotions, projectors easily lose their temper and have erratic mood swings. They can oscillate between love and hate within minutes. Don a man who had been married to a projector for 13 years, exemplifies this. He received irate and lengthy emails from his wife stating that she would "never talk" to him again and that she was "blocking" him from her email. Yet, within two hours, she was emailing him again, calmly asking him to "let the dogs out" when he got home. Elane received a text message from her husband stating, "I hope you had a good day," but received another text within fifteen minutes which angrily stated, "Suck my cock!" The very nature of a personality disorder is what allows this type of behavior to persist.

Personality disordered individuals lack insight, and are unable to take responsibility for their behaviors and actions. Equipped with a sense of entitlement, they truly believe most things are the other person's fault and they feel justified in their desire to "teach" the recipient how to be a better person. Due to projective identification, they perceive their partner as "bad" and in need of control and discipline. Without this "bad item" within the recipient's character to control, the undesirable traits would remain within the projector. They would become insecure and emotionally unbalanced, even turning to substance abuse at these times in attempt to regulate themselves. Therefore, unconsciously, it is of paramount importance for them to control the recipient, so they can protect themselves psychologically.

Stanton Samenow, a prominent researcher in the area of personality disorders, particularly anti-social personality disorders, was the first to articulate a phenomenon he referred to as "the victim stance." This stance is almost always present in an individual with a personality disorder because, as previously mentioned, it is too difficult for them to assign responsibility or blame to themselves. As a technique to avoid this, they often manipulate the situation to make it look as if they were the one at a disadvantage. A familiar phrase heard in therapy is, "After all I have done for you, and this is how you repay me?" dramatic sobs or angry voice inflections often accompany this statement. The projector is quick to point out all they have done for the recipient, even if these endeavors are self-serving. For example, a husband obsessed with his career might say to his wife, "I've done all of this for *you*." A person who is not a recipient might find these assertions comical, however, the recipient immediately feels guilt, falling for the manipulative tactic and often repeating it to others to reinforce the projector and her own stupidity for daring to challenge him.

Don's case, also exemplifies the projector's tendency to manipulate the situation. His wife, had claimed to suffer from several unexplained illnesses during their marriage. During the proceedings, she asked the court to allow her to act as her own attorney in order to save her the physical and emotional "stress" of finding her own attorney. Eventually because her illnesses could not be substantiated, she was no longer allowed to act as her own counsel. However, for those several months she had unlimited access to the information Don provided his attorney.

Projectors exhibit a substantial lack of empathy for recipients. They perceive the recipient as flawed and subhuman. The recipient becomes a possession or an object and is treated as such. In some cases, particularly with dependent personality disorders, the recipient is treated like a servant who is obligated to take care of the projector's wishes. The projector believes their needs take precedent over other responsibilities in the recipient's life. This translates to sexual relationships as well.

The recipient is treated as a vehicle for the projector's sexual satisfaction, and as a vehicle, is objectified and treated as if they do not have feelings or emotions. The projector feels entitled to demand sex with the recipient despite the recipient's feelings about the situation. For recipients the feeling of being treated like a sexual object for else's satisfaction, is humiliating. It is this shame that leads them to becoming completely uninterested in sex with their partner. Yet, the projector often finds ways to coerce them into intercourse. The projector will satisfy their sexual impulses without caring whether the recipient wants to have sex with them or not. In group therapy, the members would often ask, "How can someone want to have sex with someone who doesn't want to have sex with them?" The answer is simple, a projector puts their own wishes, needs and desires ahead of the recipient's because they believe the recipient is far less important than they.

Elane and her husband took their children to Indianapolis for a weekend. It was rare that they had time to travel, so Elane was fairly excited. Unfortunately, their first night in town, Elane came down with the flu. She raced to the bathroom to vomit every five minutes for hours. At about 4:00am, she kneeled down in front of the toilet to throw up felt something warm soaking through the knees of her pajama pants. She realized she was kneeling in a puddle of urine. Her husband had gotten up and urinated all over the bathroom floor around the toilet. Too sick and weak to unpack another pair of pajamas, Elane returned to bed soaked in her husband's urine. She was not surprised that he could care less how she might be affected by his carelessness, even at her weakest moment.

The belief that one's own feelings count more than anyone else's is another hallmark of a personality disorder. A personality disorder usually develops in infancy or toddlerhood and is sometimes the result of trauma. Trauma may include experiences such as sudden and prolonged separations from primary attachment figures, sexual or physical abuse, neglect, or parental loss. Persistent and intense shame in toddlerhood triggers the child's need to develop a defense mechanism against this intolerable feeling. Any sort of trauma can causes feelings of deep shame, and the child's first psychological stance against this overwhelming feeling is to internalize the blame. For example, it is common for a child whose parents are getting a divorce to take on the blame. Often, this comes out in therapy, with statements, such as; "If I had picked up my toys and been nice to my sister, mommy and daddy would still be together." Or in cases of physical abuse, children often say, "If I had done what my mom said, she wouldn't have had to burn me."

Psychologically, it is almost impossible for small children to see fault in their parents, especially if their attachment to them is insecure to begin with, as is common in cases of physical and sexual abuse. This resistance to perceive their parents as "bad" is a survival mechanism. Infants are born with biological instincts to attract and maintain a bond with their caregiver, and are neurologically programmed to do so. Therefore, when their caregiver does something to threaten that bond, the small child is prone to blaming themselves rather than finding fault in their caregiver.

This internalization of "bad" is the beginning of the projective identification process.

In some cases, the trauma might not be as blatant as physical or sexual abuse, yet, if the caregiver disciplines using shame, a personality disorder can develop. While using intense shame to degrade a child into submission is not a common practice anymore due to newer parenting guidelines, unfortunately, it once was. In the past, parents used to say things such as, "You are a bad boy," rather than, "You made a bad choice." Typically, a parent who uses shame as a constant element in their relationship with their child, is also highly critical of the child. The continuous barrage of criticism and feelings of intense shame causes a small child to internalize these negative feelings, which, as stated before, is the first step in the projective identification process and can lead to the child developing a personality disorder.

The feelings of intense shame that are internalized, are so painful for the child that a split can occur within the self. Instead of processing these feelings by expressing them and accessing help with them from an adult, the child unconsciously splits these parts of himself off and denies their existence. These feelings do exist however, and continually bubble to the surface unconsciously. Yet, because they are unconscious and partially denied or split off, they are acted on in a maladaptive manner rather than expressed. Often, they begin using the process of projective identification to rid these bad feelings from themselves. In a lot of cases these intolerable feelings come through in severe and aggressive behaviors including bullying.

There is an important distinction to make between individuals with personality disorders and projectors. All aggressive projectors have personality disorders, however, not all personality disordered individuals aggressively project. The likelihood of a personality disordered individual becoming a projective identifier increases dramatically if their primary caregiver in infancy is a projector. This is illustrated in the article, "Ghosts in the Nursery" by Selma Friedburg. In this article on infant mental health, there are several case vignettes that illustrate how a mother's unconscious childhood experience becomes the medium through which she understands her baby. One particular article tells the story of a mother who had endured several life threatening traumas as a child. She went on to tell her own baby, "I'm going to beat you." Later she went a step further saying, "I might kill you someday." This woman had split off feelings about her own childhood experiences, and projected them onto her baby. Frequently, mothers who are projectors experience their infants as being dangerous towards them and perceive their baby as wanting to punish them.

In therapy, mothers who are projectors often refer to their babies as if they are intentionally "out to get" them. One mother stated, "This little bitch loves to keep me up at night." Or when their infant cries, they believe the baby is doing so to purposefully to upset them instead of a signal that he/she is wet or hungry or cold. When mothers project onto their child, they act and treat the infant differently than they would normally. Believing that their baby has malicious intentions provokes the mother to interact with the baby defensively and perhaps even with hostility. Separations from the baby may be experienced as a relief by the mother because she is escaping the infant's persecutory advances, thus separations become more frequent and prolonged.

The mother's unconscious negativity towards her infant is felt and experienced by the baby. The child is left in prolonged negative states without soothing or nurturing and eventually will internalize these negative conditions. Melanie Klein referred to this as "the bad breast", a situation where the infant internalizes the negative images of his mother. The infant adopts defense mechanisms to cope with these feelings. Chances are if the hostility continues, the infant might utilize aggressive projective identification to cope with the negative and intolerable images of himself.

The infant adopts defense mechanisms to cope with these feelings. Chances are if the hostility continues, the infant will utilize aggressive projective identification to escape the negative and intolerable images of him/herself. The projective identification defense mechanism becomes entrenched in the child's character and is the "go to" defense whenever the child feels insecure or "less than." The child becomes somewhat of a bully or a mean girl as the projective identification dynamic is rooted in their character and continues to transpire in their adult relationships. Their fate is sealed and they forever become projectors.

It is important to note that Projectors may emphasize one "style" over another. For example, some projectors may utilize manipulation more than intimidation. Some may use power and control over manipulation.

The projector's style usually corresponds with their particular personality disorder. For example, a dependent personality disorder will utilize manipulation and control over bullying. A projector with borderline personality disorder will use manipulation, control and bullying. Whereas, an antisocial personality disorders will use bullying, coercion, and intimidation as their primary tactics.

Gender also influences the projector's style of projective identification. For example, a woman with a Borderline Personality Disorder, may utilize manipulation and control without bullying. Often, a female projector will criticize and condemn the recipient for not making enough money to support their family. Designating the recipient as the "provider" because of his gender, they believe they are being "victimized" somehow because the projector isn't providing them with things that other people might have. It is usually this type of projector that will spend without conscious and have multiple credit cards and balances because they feel entitled to buy what they want, despite the reality of their financial situation. This type of spending is different from the recipient who has debt because they feel guilty and ashamed for their spending, yet are unsure of how to modify it. A female borderline projector feels entitled to spend and blames the debt on their partner's inability to make enough money.

In cases where the projector has a dependent personality disorder, and is a male, the use of control and manipulation to maintain the recipient in a subservient role is prevalent. The recipient is treated like a servant, obligated to take care of the projector's every wish and need. The projector believes their needs take precedence over other responsibilities in the recipient's life, and uses projective identification to manipulate the recipient into this role. They use a victim stance in order to avoid handling the responsibilities that they think are beneath them and often avoid maintaining employment because they believe they are "above" most positions. This keeps the recipient "working for them," so to speak.

In essence, the bullying techniques utilized by projectors are the most obvious and acute, but many projectors employ control based on their gender and type of personality disorder. Each of these styles and tendencies occurs within the projective identification dynamic which intensifies their power and continually devalues the recipient.

CHECKLIST

Is your partner a projector?

Projectors may emphasize one "style" over another. For example, some projectors may utilize manipulation more than intimidation/bullying. Some may use power and control over manipulation. The projector's style usually corresponds with their particular personality disorder. For example, a dependent personality disorder will utilize manipulation over bullying, and a borderline personality disorder will utilize manipulation, control, and bullying. Whereas, an antisocial personality disorder will use bullying, coercion, and intimidation as their primary tactics.

1. Does your partner have erratic mood swings?

2. Does your partner blame you for their problems?

3. Does your partner speak to you with commands and demands?

4. Does your partner repeatedly make backhanded comments to you?

5. Is your partner incapable of having an adult discussion with you, without inserting degrading jokes or demeaning commentary?

6. Does your partner objectify you sexually?

7. Does your partner exploit your weaknesses and highlight your flaws in order to make you feel incompetent; with the goal of controlling some of your responsibilities?

8. Does your partner exploit your weaknesses in a way that makes you think no one else could possibly want you?

9. Does your partner devalue your job, your friends, your family, and your hobbies?

10. Does your partner frequently play the victim, feigning illness or emotional hardship because of you?

11. Does your partner talk negatively about you to mutual acquaintances without your knowledge?

12. Does your partner only apologize when he/she is left with no other option, and the apology is insincere, and the behavior or attitude he apologized for is resurrected within hours of the apology?

13. Does your partner continually attempt to make you out to be the "bad guy," particularly with your children?

14. Does your partner dismiss what you say as if you are invisible?

15. Does your partner look at you and treat you with disgust?

16. Does your partner compliment your achievements in front of others, but never at home?

17. Does your partner make unwanted sexual advances (groping) in front of others to demonstrate his dominance over you?

18. Does your partner call you names, yell obscenities, or tell you to "shut up" on a regular basis?

19. Have you ever felt unsafe or afraid of your partner due to the intensity of their rage?

If you answered "Yes" to 13 out of 19,
your partner is most likely a projector.

Chapter 4

THE RECIPIENT

The recipient is the vessel for the projector, and a willing participant in the unconscious exchange of dysfunction. Unintentionally embodying parts of the projector's personality, the recipient imitates these traits as their own, causing them to instantaneously feel insecure. In cases of aggressive projective identification, this can be debilitating. Introjection or internalization, can also be healthy ways of relating and identifying with people. Introjection is the process in which individuals incorporate characteristics of another person, into their own psyche unconsciously. In fact, famed psychologist Sigmund Freud who identified introjection, believed it was a necessary process in a child's development especially during infancy and toddlerhood.

For example, it is common for four year old boy to identify with his father, unconsciously taking on or "introjecting" parts of his father. His mother might ask the toddler what he wants to eat for dinner and his response could be, "I want what dad is having." He might also parade around the house in his father's shoes and tie pretending he is going to work like his dad. The same is true for a little girl, who spends time in her mommy's closet trying on her shoes and clothes, playing dress up. Elane told a story in therapy which illustrates this positive introjection. Elane's daughter, Lisa, has hazel eyes and Elane has green. One day, Lisa said to Elane, "Mom, I have green eyes like you, right?" Elane said, "Well, you have beautiful hazel eyes and mine are more of a greenish color." Lisa looked at her and exclaimed, "Yes, but we BOTH have white eyeballs!" The desire to be like her mom is actually Lisa introjecting images of her mother into her feminine identity.

When a part of the projective identification dynamic, introjection becomes negative rather than positive. The unconscious material being projected onto the recipient is detrimental and toxic. It is the shameful and worthless feelings of the projector that are experienced in the recipient, as if they originated in the recipient. The recipient immediately feels vulnerable and insecure in the projectors presence, which fuels the aggressive projector and allows him/her to use the tactics previously described to gain emotional control of the recipient.

How does an individual develop the propensity to introject the type of negative material that ties them to a projector? In most cases, it is not because they have personality disorders. They are able to take responsibility for themselves, in fact, in many situations they overly take responsibility. They are often viewed by others as "people pleasers" because they put people's needs before their own. They have the capacity for insight and self-awareness, and many recipient's struggle in painful relationships, constantly analyzing their own behaviors in order to deduce why things are going wrong. Often, because they have the capacity for self-reflection, they take on the blame for conflicts in their relationships even when they are not at fault. Recipients also have a strong sense of empathy for their fellow human beings, as they readily relate to the plight of the devalued. Unfortunately, this contributes to their disadvantage within the projective identification dynamic because the projector often plays the victim, exploiting the recipient's compassion.

There is no doubt that a recipient's self-esteem is compromised before entering the dysfunctional dynamic. Otherwise, they would not be so easily reeled in. Once they are entrapped in the aggressive projective dynamic, it is extremely difficult to break free. Although a recipient's sense of self may not be as durable as others, it is far more stable than the projector's. As previously stated, a recipient's psyche is less fragile and more evolved then the projector's, allowing them the capacity for insight, empathy, self-awareness, self-reflection, and accountability. Yet, it is these characteristics combined with a low self-esteem that seem to make the recipient vulnerable.

While low self-esteem is a factor amongst the recipient's personality that makes them vulnerable, there seems to be more to the equation. Many recipients have been involved in the projective identification dynamic for years, continually finding themselves in toxic friendships and abusive relationships. They are consistently taken advantage of and manipulated. Like most psychological phenomenon, it is fair and logical to conclude that a recipient becomes a recipient, because of early childhood experiences with this dynamic. They do not use splitting as a defense mechanism, and it is safe to conclude that recipients did not have personality disordered parents, as projectors do in many cases. Yet, they did experience profound and repeated projective identification as a child, and because of these experiences, developed a vulnerability and a propensity to repeat it in adulthood. It is safe to assume that if the mother, or primary caregiver, was not the projector, it most likely was the father or perhaps the absence of a father.

The mystery of an absent or non-involved parent creates anxiety within the child, and often the child will create defensive fantasies about why the parent is not with them. Frequently they will internalize blame, and believe they are deficient, finding themselves the cause for the abandonment. This can lead to a wounded and vulnerable self-esteem. The continuous wish or desire for the absent parent's love can become a constant longing which is internalized. In adulthood, they may become involved with a partner who repeatedly abandons them emotionally (projector), as this is the familiar dynamic that they have come to know as love. If they are encouraged to deal with these painful feelings from childhood and receive support, they are likely to break the repetition. If not, they are vulnerable to repeat their childhood experiences by becoming involved with a projector.

Sally had been married twenty years and had three beautiful children. Yet, projective identification was at work in this union. For years she had been criticized by her husband for not finishing college, for having a previous marriage that ended in a divorce, etc. When she decided to go to college and establish a career, he continually complained that her plan was adversely affecting the kids and he was spending more money on her education then it was worth. He refused to discuss any topics of interest to her, allowing only a dialogue about how expensive her schooling was and how her new career was a hardship for the family. He would frequently lose his temper, yelling degradations at her, and blame her for all of the family's problems. Occasionally, he would become so enraged that he would become physically intimidating, getting very close to her face during arguments while he yelled disrespectful comments.

In therapy when the discussion turned to Sally's family, she stated that her father had reprimanded her for not complying with her husband. He criticized her for wanting to end the marriage, stating, "You're not going to make it very far on your own" and "What do you want, a third marriage?" He was in obvious support of her husband, which lends credibility to the possibility that a recipient may become a recipient, due to a parent who was a projector. It also indicates that projectors may stick together when they have a common recipient. Just as the projector has techniques aimed at keeping a recipient an active participant in the projective identification dynamic, a recipient also utilizes techniques which keep them involved.

The first technique is to pacify their partner. They believe if they stroke their partner's ego, they will be avoiding a verbal onslaught because they will keep the projector appeased. Sometimes, they will go out of their way to show the projector that they are subservient. A case of this that transpired was with a patient, Ann. Ann was involved in an intense projective identification with her husband. Although she had a PhD, functioned at a high level at a local university, and was also an incredible mother, Ann allowed herself to be ushered out of her parenting role by her husband. He criticized her parenting and quit his job to stay home with the kids while Ann worked to support the family. Instead of sharing the parenting responsibilities when she got home from work, he relegated her to the cooking and cleaning, claiming that he was a better parent for the kids. Ann willingly complied.

Ann first attended therapy with her husband, Chris, and their four year old son Ben. Ben was anxious about toilet training and was pooping in a pull up. Chris took the lead bringing Ben to session, yet, was unwilling to hear any of the suggestions about how to help Ben at home. He became enraged and terminated his son's therapy after the third session. Ann was against terminating the therapy, but was not willing to counter her husband's wishes, so she followed his lead. During their short time in therapy, Ann had commented on her husband's patterns in relationships, his employment, and his dominating character. It seemed evident that he may have a personality disorder.

Two years later, Ann returned to therapy without her son or her husband. She had a second child who was two. Chris continued to marginalize her at home, doing his best to isolate her from her children by setting her up as the "bread winner" and dictating that he do the parenting, especially for the eldest son who he repeatedly referred to as "his child." Ann still found ways to steal away warm moments with her sons, and continued to encourage her husband to get a job. When her husband was forced to travel for a few weeks out of the month, Ann became the full time parent, and during his absence it became clear to her that she wasn't a "lousy mother" after all. She found herself supporting and nurturing her sons in such a way that they began achieving several age appropriate developmental tasks, such as sleeping in their own beds, appropriate toilet training, and engaging in positive social interactions with their peers.

She brought Ben back to therapy, and he seemed to have a much different demeanor then two years prior. He appeared happy, was cheerful, and talked about his new abilities with pride and confidence. Ann began to realize that her husband had encouraged her to believe she was incompetent in other ways as well. For example, he insisted on managing the money because he believed her to be "incompetent" in this area, despite the fact that Ann had never had financial problems before or during the marriage. Slowly, Ann began to realize that she was exceptionally competent. As she gained confidence she started to intensely resent her husband who became increasingly possessive and controlling. Eventually, she decided to file for divorce. Although the process was difficult, she and Chris agreed on joint custody. She disclosed she loves being a mom to her sons, who are both thriving.

In addition to putting themselves in subservient roles to preserve peace in the relationship, recipients actively seek out projectors, just as projectors actively seek out recipients. Again, this is an unconscious courtship which originated with their own parents in childhood. Inherently intuitive, recipients are very sensitive to the moods and emotions of others, particularly projectors. Insecure and vulnerable in relationships, a recipient may pick up on the subtle negative feeling states of another; automatically taking responsibility for it. They believe that, somehow, the negative emotions the other person is experiencing, are their fault, and therefore are justifiably directed at them. They quickly act, making contact with the projector in order to compliment or stroke this person's ego, in order to ensure a good standing in the relationship. Yet, it is this initiation of contact with the projector that begins the projective identification cycle, and immediately places the recipient in a devalued position. Due to this, it is unclear who *actually* starts the projective identification dynamic; the recipient or the projector.

In lay terms this is often referred to as "ass kissing", and although it can set a projective dynamic in motion, it is also a tactic for the recipient to maintain their role as devalued object. In other words, they value the projector and the relationship more then they value themselves. As a part of undervaluing themselves, recipients often get into the habit of self-depreciating humor. In the case of Ann, she often chuckled in session and referred to herself as a "dummy." When reminded that she was not, she realized how many times a day she would say that about herself. She also recalled referring to herself as a dummy to her husband and believed she was doing so in order to avoid a possible altercation.

After gaining this insight, she recounted an experience she had with a colleague a week earlier. She supportively brought to his attention a mistake he had made. She described being "shocked and dumbfounded" by his response. He apologized sincerely and asked her for her guidance on how to avoid the mistake again. When he left her office, he complimented her work. Ann was astonished. She couldn't remember a time in her marriage when she was ever treated with that kind of respect and dignity, nor could she remember a time when her husband apologized to her. However, it was also she who had been referring to *herself* as a "dummy", in her relationship.

In a complex relationship that is based upon a web of dysfunction, how does one free themselves? It is partially the recipient's capacity for insight and introspection that can free them. As discussed, most projectors have personality disorders that prevent them from gaining insight into their patterns of behaviors. Arrested emotionally, they have minimal hope of ever maturing or evolving. The recipient, on the other hand, has the capacity for insight, empathy, and self-awareness, thus embodying the necessary skills to continue to grow emotionally. With one participant evolving and the other at an emotional standstill, an impasse in the relationship is inevitable. Even if the recipient is a willing participant in this dynamic, and seems to be invested in it, the experience of being continually mistreated will be realized eventually. Dignity is a human right. When it is purposefully taken from someone, it is felt deeply in their core. Whether they deny it or tolerate it for five weeks or fifty years, it is inevitable that they will eventually fight back, fight hard and they will roar.

There may even be quiet roars through the entire relationship. The feeling of being humiliated, dismissed and disrespected would enrage anyone. It is only natural that the recipient retaliate once and awhile. Yet, of course, the retaliation is met with additional degradation and verbal onslaught, so unfortunately there is no immediate resolution. After the altercation, it is the recipient, not the projector, who has remorse for coming "unglued". The projector, who is incapable of feeling responsible for any of their behaviors, makes it a point to highlight the recipient's anger during the fight and blame them, accusing them of being out of control. Recipients overly take accountability for their actions in order to save their partner from feeling the burden of responsibility, they succumb and plead for forgiveness.

A recipient is vulnerable to taking on the unconscious material of another, and because of this, their capacity for empathy is great. They have a sixth sense for another's pain and can respond in an exceedingly compassionate manner. Yet, it is this capacity for empathy that also makes them vulnerable to the pathological projective identifications which can be detrimental and damaging to them. This explains why recipients often take on acts of intense humanitarianism, but can also be dismantled quickly when they encounter a projector, who uses the gift of empathy against them.

While recipients have a more compassionate demeanor in comparison to the classic projector, it is important to note, they are not saints. They can sometimes act selfishly and or aggressively, but these tendencies usually occur in the face of a projection. Their basic nature is to empathize, understand, connect, and stay attuned to others. They are usually creative and humorous as they are open to the depth and color of humanness. Yet, their deep and sensitive character is the perfect burial ground for a projectors toxic material, and the projection can quickly deduce a recipient into a puddle. The recipient sincerely believes that they are a worthless human being who can do nothing right when they are in the midst of a toxic projection. They attribute their past successes to luck and readily take in any negative feedback from the environment as evidence that they are useless.

When educated about projectors a recipient can avoid becoming involved in these types of projections. If the interaction is unavoidable, they may prepare themselves for a projection, which can make a significant difference in the effectiveness in the projective identification relationship.

CHECKLIST
Are you a recipient?

1. Do you have a low self-esteem?

2. Do you find yourself apologizing more than others?

3. Do you continually worry about what other people think about you?

4. Are you surprised and flattered when people like you?

5. Do you automatically blame yourself for problems during interactions, and overly take responsibility for them?

6. Do you stroke other people's egos in order to keep yourself in good standing with them?

7. Do you continually use self-deprecating humor?

8. Do you believe you are so flawed in one particular area, i.e.: overweight, unattractive, inability to manage money, inability to stay organized, that you believe no one but your partner will want you?

9. Are you compassionate and empathic?

10. Do you readily defend the devalued, disadvantaged, and the disenfranchised?

11. Would you give your life for another human being without a second thought?

12. Do you continually put your needs and wishes secondary to your partners?

13. Do you feel anxious prior to interactions with your partner at the end of the day?

14. You would not allow anyone to be bullied in your presence, but you find yourself being bullied, back stabbed, or taken advantage of frequently in your relationships.

If you answered YES to 10 out of 14 of these questions,
you are a recipient.

Chapter 5

THE SPELL

The depression a recipient feels during a projection is different from the more common form of situational depression. When a loss occurs, such as the death of a family member, loss of a job, or a loved one falling ill… negative emotions such as grief, disappointment, fear, powerlessness, and hopelessness can overwhelm a person. These are debilitating emotions, and can be challenging to cope with, but with the support and love of friends and family, these situations can also sometimes bring people closer.

Experiencing a projection is a very different type of depression because the person's sense of self is turned against them. It is similar to having an auto immune disorder of the soul. The prominent emotions are not grief and disappointment, they are self-loathing and self-doubt. The recipient condemns themselves, and feelings of shame and guilt reign supreme. The destructive element about this dynamic is that the recipient has no knowledge that these feelings belong to someone else. They unconsciously claim them, and wage a psychological war on their own spirit. Despite the intellectual knowledge that the projector is not a healthy individual, they unconsciously and intuitively believe they are the "bad" person in the relationship and the projector is the "good" person. Outside of the projection, they are aware on every level that the projector is pathological in nature.

While enduring a projection, the recipient cannot accept support or reassurance because they are consumed with self-contempt, which isolates them from other people. This creates a vicious cycle of shame and disconnectedness from friends and family who would ordinarily be their support system. Projections isolate the recipient emotionally, so they are not easily escaped. It can take days for a projection to dissipate. During this time, it is common for the recipient to berate themselves and question whether they can survive without the projector. They feel so deprived, they perceive the projector as the stronger party and they are vulnerable to "throwing in the towel." By surrendering to the projector, and returning to the destructive dynamic, they believe they will find relief from their own self deprivation. Yet, it is the projector that is conjuring up these feelings in the recipient. If the recipient can tolerate painful projections as they continue to gain independence from the projector, their confidence and momentum will develop. "Keep fighting," was the phrase Elane's friend would repeat to her in the midst of a virulent projection. She was well aware that Elane could not accept compliments or reassurance about herself when she was bewitched by a projection. The simple phrase "keep fighting," was about Elane's actions, not validation about who she was. This was the type of encouragement Elane could accept, metabolize, and use to move forward.

As the recipient works to build emotional distance from their partner, the projections become less noxious and frequent. They do not evaporate entirely immediately. Depending on how strong the recipient's confidence is at the time of the encounter, they may be susceptible to a projection. An awareness of this phenomenon will help the recipient protect themselves.

In essence, the experience of a projection is a type of depression, but it is a different animal then the typical situational depression. Having knowledge and information that a noxious projection can do dreadful things to a recipient's sense of self may help, in addition to knowing that they are not alone in this experience. Every day clients enter therapy who are experiencing and enduring painful projections. It is more common than realized and needs to be correctly identified, acknowledged and treated.

Chapter 6

BREAKING THE CHAINS

CASE STUDY FILES

The attempt to end a relationship that is based upon projective identification, can be as besieging as climbing out of quick sand. It takes great emotional investment to have entered this type of relationship, yet, it is emotional distance that will successfully end the destructive dynamic. Power is lost if both partners are no longer emotionally invested. The recipient may not care for the projector anymore after enduring such mistreatment, but the projector usually has additional ammunition up his or her sleeve to keep the recipient emotionally involved. Examples include; the children that they have together, investments that they share, friendships, and family members that they both have relationships with. Aware that the recipient is innately compassionate, the projector may also try to use themselves and their wellbeing to keep the recipient devoted.

Elane illustrates a projector's attempts to keep the recipient invested. After lengthy and critical deliberation, Elane decided to leave her husband.

Desperate to keep her emotionally involved, her husband said he was planning on contacting their adopted children's biological parents, to inform them that she was thinking about filling for divorce. Elane, who had raised two special needs infants on her own, with little to no help aside from financial support from her husband, was sick with worry and immediately reconsidered staying in the relationship. In the case of Salle, whose case often times parallels Elane's, we find examples of a projector using his own wellbeing to keep the recipient invested. Shortly after Sally informed her husband she was filling for divorce, he oscillated between being intensely angry and very dramatic. One night he spent three hours on the telephone with an emergency crisis worker. Sally could hear him continually sobbing and crying very loudly during the duration of this call. Worried, she checked on him several times, but he waved her away. Finally, desperate to help him, she approached him and attempted to soothe him. At that point, he grabbed his chest and stumbled, crying out that he was having chest pains. She immediately rushed him to the hospital and stayed with him through the night. The tests returned inconclusive and the doctors hypothesized that he experienced a panic attack. Sally, who was consumed with worry and fear that she may be the cause of her husband's health problems, delayed filling for divorce.

Elane found herself at financial risk when her husband threatened to shut down her credit card after informing him she wanted out of the relationship. He refused to give her money and followed her around the house berating her, saying things like, "Do you really think YOU deserve child support?" He perceived Elane as more of a possession then a human being, and treated her as such, so felt justified in his belief that he could humiliate and degrade her. Elane, who also believed she "owed" him because he had paid of some of her debt during the marriage, subjected herself to this continuous degradation. He would frequently say to their children with Elane present, "This is MY house" and "These are MY cars." He would accentuate to their small children that he paid for, and owned everything. These assertions also were being used to insinuate he owned Elane. He excluded her from any involvement in the finances and constantly reminded of her inability to manage money, so she remained clueless. In one session, she described her attorney's shock when she told him she had no idea what her husband had in their savings account or what they owned in stock or had in their other accounts.

When Elane became more serious about the divorce, her husband tried another avenue in using money as a tool to keep her. This time he offered to buy her a condo in which she could live for free, as long as she did not move forward with the divorce. However once she did move forward, her husband's projective habits effected the proceedings. Eager to impress the neighbors, because their prestige had impressed him, Elane's husband ensured they knew of the financial arrangements within their separation. He went so far as giving Elane her settlement money earlier than required. With that, he made sure she purchased a new house nearby, then proceeded to brag to the neighbors that he bought her that home. His ability to interweave Elane into games built off of his insecurities were still apparent.

Unfortunately, children are often the most common resource a projector has in maintaining the recipient's investment in the relationship. In the case of Molly, after she and her husband were separated, her husband called their daughter every night and talked to her for hours, though he rarely spent time with her. The projector, as with friends and relatives, will try to get the children to align with him/her against the recipient. They will buy them elaborate gifts and adorn them with affection, yet before the separation with the recipient, the projector rarely gave their children a moments worth of attention or could tolerate a difficult moment with their child.

Attempts to put the children in the middle of the crumbling relationship in order to keep the recipient invested was common in Elane's situation. During her divorce process, her husband often involved his children in debates. When Elane picked her children up from his house, her husband often followed the children and Elane out to her car. He would then hang on the kid's windows with his elbows resting on the car so she could not leave. Often times he would engage the kids in conversations about something negative Elane may be doing. Elane calmly reminded her husband that it was inappropriate to involve the children in adult matters, but to no avail. Her husband continued to address the kids stating, " Right guys, didn't you hear mom say that?" Upset that he was dragging her children into an adult situation, she pleaded with him to stop, yet he refused. She reported being so upset that she literally had to get in her car and inch down the driveway until he gave up.

Days later, Elane's husband asked to take the kids to a football game. Elane agreed. Her husband invited her as well, she ignored the invitation in order to avoid an argument, and responded with "The kids would love to go." A few days later, he told her he was glad she agreed to go. Shocked that he had interpreted her lack of a response as a "Yes," she apologized for the miscommunication and informed him she would not be going. Angry and insisting that she must go, he texted her multiple times a day stating, "You have to go, the kids need you to go." "The kids need to see us getting along. "Be a good mom and go to the game with us."

After trying to coerce her into going, he stated, "If you don't go, you will owe me $350 for the tickets." Elane stood her ground, however a week before the game the kids told her, "Daddy said you aren't going to the game because you don't want to be with us. He said you promised to go, but now you don't feel like going." On another occasion, her children told her that "Daddy only buys us presents if we tell him what you do." Soon after, when both Elane and her husband were at their children's soccer practice standing next to each other, her husband called his son off the field over to him. He reached into his pocket and took out a child support check and said, "Give that to your mother." who was standing less than a foot away.

The most painful and manipulative attempt to put their kids in the middle of their relationship involved their first day of kindergarten. Her husband told her that he wanted to see the children on their first day of school, and she agreed. At this point he was not allowed at her residence because he had been verbally abusive to her several times, so she told him the time and location of the bus stop. She told her kids that their dad would be at the bus stop that morning to wish them well on their first day of school. Yet, she was surprised when he did not come. Her daughter, got on the bus teary eyed, not understanding why her dad didn't come. Elane comforted her as best she could, but was crushed that her daughter and son left for their first day of school with tears in their eyes. Later, her husband texted her and told her that he didn't show up because he didn't feel like standing on the street. She was confused and told him that all the parents stand on the street at the bus stop. He continued to insist that she had made him feel uncomfortable and he wasn't going to wait on the street. He exhibited no remorse for hurting the kid's feelings. She pleaded with him not to blame her, but to take responsibility. He ignored her and at the visit with his children that night, he told them that it was Elane's fault he did not come.

A few months later, Elane was eating dinner with her children. Earlier that week, she helped her son with his art project which was based on what the kids wanted to be when they grew up. Her five year old son told her that he was glad that she had reminded him that since the age of two, he had wanted to be a police officer when he grew up. He was so adamant about it that Elane had arranged for a cousin to take him to the police station where he worked to give her son a tour. At the dinner table her son said, "Mom, I want to be a police officer, but dad wants me to be a spy right now." Elane nodded and said that spies are a special type of police officer, but her son interrupted her and said, "But spies aren't real." Elane interjected going on to explain, "Spies are very real, they work for the government in secret ways." Her son looked at her and said, "That's good, because I am a spy right now and I spy on you and you don't even know it." Stunned and very aware that her husband had been questioning her children about her personal life, she calmly said, "We'll, that's good practice if you want to be a police officer -- it's a good thing I have nothing to hide," and she winked at him. Once again, Elane realized that her husband was more concerned about controlling her then the psychological welfare of his son, who he continually put in the middle of their divorce.

Utilizing mutual friends is also a way to keep the recipient invested. The tactics are similar to those used in childhood bullying. Elane was informed by an old neighbor that her husband had been sending out mass texts to all of their old neighbors about her. When Elane asked what was said, her friend's husband stated, "They are so nasty that I erase them immediately because I don't want my kids to accidentally see them."

Elane had a male friend who had become a reliable source of comfort during the divorce. She began to look at the idea of dating him when the proceedings were over. However, the distortions, lies, and exaggerations that her husband had made up about her relationship with him ruined that prospect. Salacious and graphic, her husband tore into her character and degraded her publicly to all of their friends. Their old friends would barely talk to Elane when they ran into her at the grocery store and some, joined in the bullying. Two women who were wives of her husband's friends (and also projectors) were on her golf team, and gossiped about Elane when she was not able to go to practice. Eventually, they convinced the captain to ask her to leave the team. Her husband's friends spread rumors about Elane so pervasively that they were in contact with all of her new neighbors. Luckily, Elane's new neighbors were not projectors and refused to participate in the projection, yet, Elane felt like he was going to bully her right out of town. She often contemplated going back to him just to end the witch hunt.

Escaping the projector's grip is difficult and can be painful, so painful, in fact, that the recipient must have support. If the recipient can find other recipients to talk to and be with, the chances are greater that they will be fortified enough to leave the projector. Yet, because the projector has aligned people against the recipient, finding others to understand and support them may be difficult.

Another way to understand the projector's attempts to align people with themselves and against the recipient, is by understanding it as a "group projective identification". The group projection occurs in the social realm, and attracts projectors who join in and spread the "hate" for the recipient. The recipient, who is vulnerable to projective identification, can become extremely disempowered feeling like Elane, who stated in session; "The whole world hates me." Attempts by the recipient to stand up for themselves, only fuel the projector's because the recipient is engaging with them. Any engagement gives them access to the recipient, and that is what the projectors want. The recipient's most effective course of action is to ignore the projectors and continue to distance themselves from the projectors. However, because they are feel disempowered, discouraged and demoralized, it is difficult. Having their own support network including other recipients who can empathize with the recipient's plight is imperative.

Adept at influencing others, especially against the recipient, the projector is just as skilled at "brainwashing" the recipient. Already vulnerable and unsure of their own worth, recipients tend to slowly, but surely, adopt the projectors views. Their own opinions and values have been continually depreciated by the projector, so it is natural that they would begin to abandon some of their values and absorb the projectors. For example, Diane who had been married to a projector for 19 years, wanted to see her daughter, who had recently given birth. Her first grandson had arrived, and Diane was dying to meet him and visit her daughter whose delivery had been difficult. Diane's husband, who was the father and grandfather, would not allow Diane to go to the hospital. He didn't believe that family should go to the hospital. He felt it was more appropriate to wait until mom and baby were at home. Diane conceded to his wishes, believing that he was probably right.

Carrie provides another example. Carrie who had strong political beliefs, and even chose a career which was consistent with these principles. Although she kept her views private, her husband continually taunted, teased, and tortured her for her political stance. He broadcasted her beliefs to all of their mutual friends who took every opportunity to make derogatory comments to her and behind her back. After years of enduring this pressure, she conceded to her husband's wishes and changed her vote on Election Day.

The projector has a constant need to control the recipient in both action and thought. They degrade any values and beliefs that are not consistent with theirs, and pressure the recipient to think like them. Yet, this pressure does not take the form of appropriate communication or respectful dialogue. It is levied from an arrogant and superior stance, and it usually involves putting down the recipient.

A form of "thought control" is often pressed upon the children of projectors. They degrade any thought, idea, or belief that is not consistent with their own. A healthy parent should honor their child's feelings and ideas despite their differences. A parent with a strong sense of self can tolerate ideas and thoughts that are not congruent with their own, and sometimes gets a kick out of looking at the world from a different point of view. A fragile parent has to have constant validation from their children that they think like their parent because if they don't, the parent feels insecure and a loss of control. An insecure parent rejects their child if the child is "embarrassing" them by not doing exactly what they want. A secure parent understands that being a parent means their feelings and pride come secondary to their child's. They are the source of ego strength for their child and not vice versa.

Revisiting Carrie; Carrie's kids were involved in soccer at a very young age. One day, late in the season, the weather turned frigid and her son had to sit and watch his sister's game before playing in his own. When it came time to play his game, his 34 pound body was freezing, and he was hurting. Carrie encouraged him to play, reassuring him that the running would warm him up, but her son was upset. Cold and tired, he ran onto the field because of Carrie's encouragement, then off again because he was physically exhausted. This occurred multiple times during the game, Carrie's husband walked off the field disgusted at his son. Carrie, believing in the theory of finishing the race, game, match, or whatever it may be, despite adversity, encouraged her son to stick out. Although she felt it was humiliating to watch her son run off the field multiple times crying, she tolerated the embarrassment. Her son was on the field when the game ended. He finished his last soccer game without quitting because Carrie had been there to support and encourage him despite the embarrassment and drama. Her husband, who could not take the embarrassment quit on her son and walked off the field.

A projector is consumed with feeling good about themselves, they have a difficult time recognizing or acknowledging the feelings of others, which leads to a lack of empathy for other people. This lack of empathy is what allows them to bully without conscience. It is also this inability to understand and recognize how their children feel that can be detrimental to the child. They need their children to be a reflection of themselves and need their children to stroke their ego. However, children need the opposite from their parents. It's a parent's responsibility to recognize hurt, anger, and disappointed feelings within their child, and help their child feel comforted. If a parent cannot be attuned in detecting when something is amiss, that parent is too absorbed with their own feelings. In addition, if they do not notice their child struggling, they only understand the child's experience if it is consistent with how they would feel in that situation. Their perception is the only thing they will consider. This is why they feel they are always right. They cannot, and will not, honor a difference of opinion without degrading and condemning it. If their child has a different perspective or opinion, they will reject the child's feelings. The projector's inability to genuinely and authentically consider someone else's feelings is what drives them to believe they can gain total thought control over the recipient. To the projector it's a game, because they only consider their own feelings. They treat the recipient as an object to be manipulated rather than a human being to be respected.

The parent child relationship of Ashly and her mother, exemplify this. Ashly, who turned eighteen, could no longer handle the projective identification cycle she was involved in with her mother and decided to leave home. Although she thrived on her own and was happy, her mother insisted on Ashly returning home. Instead of being happy for her daughter's independence, success, and happiness, she could only consider her own feelings. In one session she stated, "It would be easier if she were dead, because at least then I could grieve for her and move on." Ashly's mom would rather have her daughter dead then outside of her emotional control. Though as her therapist I reminded her that Ashly was happy and successful, she could not stop feeling sorry for herself long enough to consider her daughter's happiness. She continually dwelled on how terrible she felt being emotionally distant from her daughter.

After years and years of projective identification, a recipient can actually lose their own identity and become dependent on the projector's perception of them as their sense of self. They begin to do and say what the projector wants in hopes of riding on the projector's coat tails for the remainder of their life. They become a minion. Hopefully, they can break free of the relationship before they lose their sense of self, dignity, voice, and passions. One way for a recipient to understand the damage to their sense of self is through other recipients.

When recipients come together in a support group format, they are able to see themselves in the other members of the group. Instead of feeling alone and isolated, they feel connected and attached to others. This feeling starts them on a pathway out of the dysfunctional interpersonal relationship. They feel useful, connected, and able to help others, which is an essential motivation for a recipient. Recipients care deeply about helping people.

An additional aspect about being a recipient which was realized from facilitating these support groups, was the quality of strength in each recipient. Although emotionally abused, and lacking self-esteem within their relationships, they were fighters outside of the relationship. Each had established a successful career, put themselves through school while raising kids and working, fought through illnesses, and never stopped evolving. They were accomplished and successful individuals, however, within their interpersonal relationship, they quickly shed their self-esteem in order to appease their projector. Equally as poignant, was their shared sense of humor, and together they were able to laugh at the idea of once being convinced they were idiots. As a group, they had the power of recognition. By looking across the room at each other, they realized how fantastic they were. They looked into a realistic mirror instead of a distorted one, and saw themselves in each other.

For years prior they had seen themselves through their projector's eyes. They saw themselves as weak, incompetent, financially irresponsible, and morally deficient. Group therapy, offered a different reflection of themselves. They mirrored each other in positive ways and reminded each other how amazing each person was. A realistic and positive self-image was reflected back to them instead of a distorted one. This experience, along with their own personal journey separating and differentiating from their dysfunctional attachment to their projector may be enough to help them leave.

Chapter 7

PROJECTIVE IDENTIFICATION

IN THE WORK PLACE

Projective identification in the context of a group can occur in the professional setting as well. Carrie, a recipient, had been employed as a speech pathologist for several years at a hospital. She operated in a specialized clinic within the hospital, which was known to have a problematic staff. There were several nurses in her department that, were "trouble makers." Yet, because they were administered by the clinics director, a fairly narcissist physician, they were somewhat protected from the larger hospitals administration team. For several years, she observed a cycle that involved several nurses aligning against one nurse, eventually, running the nurse out of the department. Once the nurse was gone, they would select another target and the pattern of group projective identification would continue.

One morning while doing her rounds, Carrie began to realize that she had become the new target. The clinic had established a protocol for discussing their patients. Each discipline had a chance to report on their progress with the patient. The primary medical personnel reported first, followed by a line of doctors and nurses, eventually leading their way to Carrie's report. When it was Carrie's turn to give her report, she noticed snickers from some of the nurses. Two scribbled notes to each other and chuckled while she was talking, and one interrupted her to contradict what she was saying. The antics continued outside of rounds as well. She was often left out of the group conversation in the break room, and would be ignored if she tried to join the conversation. On multiple occasions, the nurses would get up and leave the break room when Carrie entered. They often planned lunches and social events outside of work in front of her, yet did not include her. At one point, she was called into her manager's office to talk about her performance because the nurses had complained about her. Carrie ignored the nurses as best she could because she knew she did not have a chance of salvaging her job in the clinic if she further irritated them. However, the bullying continued and intensified. The nurses would maliciously tease her to her face, often criticizing her outfit or hair, and would refer to her in derogatory terms like "air head" or "flighty."

Although Carrie loved her job, she started to dread going to work. She became nauseous in the clinic and often had to retreat to the restroom to gain her composure. She felt depressed and anxious. Unable to tolerate the group projection, she started to believe that she was incompetent, and contemplated a change in profession. However, Carrie decided to take control of her emotions and entered therapy. After a few weeks, Carrie felt stronger and decided to remain in the profession she had enjoyed for years, but requested a transfer.

Another example involved a client named Matt. Matt was a procurement officer for his company. He had been with his company for sixteen years, and was well respected and liked by his colleagues. The day he entered therapy, he appeared distraught and anxious, stating that he had reached his, "breaking point" at work. Although he said he enjoyed his job and had positive relationships with almost everyone he worked with, he indicated that there was one particular colleague with whom he was having problems. The anxiety he was having as a result of these interactions had caused him such distress that he had "walked off the job" the prior week. He was not eating, sleeping, and had lost interest in almost everything he used to enjoy. The dread he felt at the thought of returning to work made him physically ill.

Matt said the problems with his co-worker started about a year before he entered therapy. He was unclear as to why this colleague "had it out" for him because they were both managers of departments which had very little interaction or overlap. Yet, this employee continually Called Matt to attack him about his work, most often contacting Matt on his cell phone during non-business hours. He often threatened to "get Matt fired" if Matt didn't "shape up." In addition, he contacted Matt's boss and continually referred to Matt as "lazy" and a "liar." Matt's boss, who was new to the company, defended Matt and his work, but was equally confused about the situation. After a few months, Matt's supervisor became anxious and overwhelmed with the co - workers continued attacks against Matt, so he appealed to the Vice President of the company. The vice president of the company agreed this co-worker was acting out inappropriately, but acknowledged he was being protected, by the president of the company. Although he did not go into specifics, it was obvious that the president of the company viewed this person an enforcer who kept people in line. After much thought, Matt came to the conclusion that the president was passive and may have felt the need to have a "bull dog" to compensate for his timid manner.

Once other managers heard about Matt's trouble. Several came forward and acknowledged that this co-worker had also inappropriately contacted them multiple times during off hours to criticize their work, and also threaten their jobs. He had followed the same pattern of contacting their supervisors behind their backs in order to accuse them of being "lazy" and "liars" as well. The vice president eventually contacted human resources who immediately stopped the harassment. Matt was relieved to be free of this projector and resumed his work happily. Although Matt's colleague had attempted to implement a very common strategy of a projector, which was to talk about the recipient behind his back hoping to destroy his character. Matt's projector involved *one* very powerful individual instead of using a *group*. There is strength in numbers, yet if the projector can align an extremely powerful person with them, they feel they assume that power as well.

Mary worked for a small company with several ophthalmologists and one physician who completed the clinic's eye surgeries. The company hired a young, attractive office manager who began to have fairly casual and informal conversations with the surgeon in front of Mary. It was clear to Mary they had established a special relationship. The office manager seemed to dislike Mary and began to schedule Mary for undesirable shifts and even cut her hours. When Mary eventually inquired about the changes in her schedule, the office manager stated, "If you don't like it, you can find a job elsewhere." One day when Mary was in the common area of the office suite, she overheard the office manager and doctor laughing loudly and attracting attention. When Mary walked past, she realized they were watching an instructional You Tube video about how to put on a condom using a banana as the model. Shocked and uncomfortable, Mary left the area and decided to alert the director of the clinic. Yet, because the physician supported the office manager, Mary's complaints were dismissed. Mary's schedule worsened and eventually, she felt she had no choice but to find a new job.

The group projective identifications that occur in the professional arena are again, not very different from the bully on the playground. Bullies or projectors, feel empowered if they have individuals who agree that the recipient deserves to be humiliated. The fascinating aspect about this dynamic is that the projector's followers or "minions," are not able to think critically about the situation for themselves. They are influenced so powerfully by the projection that they follow blindly, often because they are grateful they are not the victim.

In 2005 on a corner on the south side of Chicago, a boy was beat to death by two other boys while a crowd watched. Adults and teenagers witnessed a young, intelligent, vital young man, bludgeoned to death on a public street corner in the middle of the day by two other kids. No one attempted to help. If one of the adults watching would've intervened, the others probably would've joined them. Two or three adults together could have saved this young man's life. Rather, they stood and watched as if it was a show. Imagine if that was your child, and your neighbors watched as he brutally lost his life. When the patrons were interviewed, one stated, "He probably deserved it, why should I risk my own safety for a bad kid?" Whether individuals participate in the projection directly or observe it and support the violence by accepting it as status quo, they are perpetrating the cycle. They might as well have been holding the bat.

Chapter 8

THE PARENT CHILD RELATIONSHIP

This next chapter further investigates the effects projective identification can have upon the relationship between a parent and their child. A child may be a recipient for a parent who uses projective identification, and when this occurs they may fall victim to this dynamic for the remainder of their lives. The pattern of introjecting their parent's psychological baggage, is their way of protecting their parents from pain and suffering. This is an unconscious process established at a very young age. The children have an unconscious desire to save their parents from themselves.

This is demonstrated in the case of Elisha. As a freshman in college, Elisha came to her initial session severely depressed, so depressed, in fact that my immediate response was to hospitalize her. She was soft spoken and quiet, young, beautiful, and intelligent. Elisha reported that she spent most of her days crying in her dorm room. She was unable to maintain friendships or her grades. Her initial visit with me occurred on her 20th birthday, which she was planning on spending alone. As Elisha's story unfolded, it seemed evident that her father was a projector, and her mom was a recipient. She recalled her dad working unusually long hours during her childhood. "When he came home, he watched TV. We knew we couldn't interrupt his TV," Elisha said. She described sitting with her siblings and her mom at the dinner table, attempting to be quiet as not to disturb her dad, who became angry if he was interrupted. If she and her siblings became too noisy, he would repeatedly turn the volume up to make his point.

One night, when Elisha was a teenager, Elisha's mom took them out for ice cream and brought Elisha's father a sundae home. Unfortunately, the sundae was not exactly to his liking, so he began to scream and yell. Elisha and her siblings went upstairs, but her dad became so enraged that he became physically intimidating towards their mom. Elisha's older sibling went downstairs to help their mom and their dad retaliated against her sibling. After the altercations, Elisha's dad told the children, "This is what married people do." Elisha said volatility was common in their household. She remembered him frequently "getting in her face." As a little girl, she described being "very scared" of him. As a teenager, she said, "he would rip me out of bed if I didn't wake up immediately."

Elisha's relationship with her father was disheartening. In high school, she was described as an overachiever. She was a gifted student and track star, but was quiet and withdrawn, which was probably symptomatic her depression. She attempted to tell her dad about her depression on several occasions, but was ignored. Yet, he disliked her quiet and reserved qualities and would frequently lecture her about it, stating, "You need to work on being happy." He even tried to bribe her into smiling more, promising her items he knew she liked if she would smile more and act happy. Unfortunately, he was not concerned about Elisha's feelings and emotional state, his concerns were based upon about how people perceived Elisha and how that perception reflected on him. He related to Elisha as more of a possession than a human being, an object that could either enhance his self-esteem or detract from it. He wasn't able to recognize or accept that she had her own feelings.

Elisha's acceptance into a prominent university meant a lot to her father. After opening Elisha's acceptance letter, he immediately wrote a check to enroll her and rushed to the store to buy the universities flag to fly outside of his house and university paraphernalia to put on his car. However, he did not think to ask Elisha if she wanted to attend the university. She had been accepted to many outstanding schools, yet, her father did not ask her for an opinion. Again, he did not recognize that Elisha might have feelings about where she went to college as he was only capable of considering his own desires and wishes. In order to avoid the fights between her father and her mother, Elisha volunteered at a homeless shelter. She volunteered every day after school and even on the weekends as well. She became close with the director, other volunteers and the families. Though her parents did not understand her connection to the shelter, they allowed her to spend much of her time there.

As Elisha described more of her family experiences, it was evident that she was the recipient for her older sibling as well. Her older sibling, Sandra, who Elisha described as being similar to her father seemed unusually cruel to Elisha. The night before Sandra's wedding, Sandra made several cutting comments to Elisha. Hurt and confused, but unwilling to perpetuate drama at her sister's rehearsal dinner, Elisha she refrained from defending herself. That night, Sandra barged into Elisha's room and screamed and yelled at her for being "quiet" and "weak." No longer able to tolerate the onslaught, Elisha argued back. Infuriated that Elisha fought back, Sandra revoked Elisha's responsibilities as the maid of honor at the wedding. Demoralized and disappointed Elisha spent the night writing her sister a heartfelt letter in attempt to pacify the situation.

After Elisha shared this story in therapy, it was time to introduce her to method of projective identification. It was important for her to be able understand the pattern of projective identification realize how painful it can be to be for a recipient. Elisha resonated with what was described and appeared relieved to have a plan of action in removing herself from the dynamic. Elisha had been shamed and ignored for most of her childhood and had witnessed her mom being treated similarly. This, in addition, to the physical intimidation, had a dehumanizing effect. Elisha, like many recipients, was ashamed and distrustful of her own feelings and emotions, which can cause deep depression.

Anne was a single woman in her early twenties when she came to therapy. Initially, Anne presented with anxiety about a career change, but after a few sessions we began to focus on her interpersonal relationship. Anne described being "in love," for the first time but was terrified of physical intimacy. She disclosed feelings of guilt and shame about her physical desire for boyfriend. As she grappled with this conflict, she began to associate to her childhood. After asking her if she remembered experiencing this feeling of deep shame when she was young. She quietly said that she had, and began to recount one of her most painful experiences.

A talented runner, Anne had traveled to Colorado for a junior national race. The youngest member of her team at just thirteen years old, the other girls were at least a year older and already freshmen in high school. The evening before the meet, her team mates asked her to go to an amusement park with them. Excited about the prospect of going out with her friends, she begged her parents for permission to go. Her parents agreed. While at the amusement park, Anne began to realize that her team mates were more interested in meeting boys then riding the rides. Anne was nervous, but went along with the older girls. During their interactions with one group of boys their age, Anne's team mate indicated to Anne that one of the boys "liked" Anne. Shocked and dumbfounded because she considered herself less sophisticated then the other girls, she was flattered. Nervous because she had not spent one on one time with a boy, Anne tried to "be cool." She followed her friend's instructions to ride a few rides with him. After a while, she realized that she was late and frantically raced back to her hotel room.

When Anne entered the hotel room, her father was enraged. He accused her of being boy crazy and stated, "You act like a little slut!" Anne described feeling so ashamed that she couldn't breathe. She remembered crying for most of the night with her head buried underneath her pillow. The next morning she felt like someone had poured cement into her legs. During the race, she felt like she could barely pick up her feet. She ran the worst race of her life. For months after the meet, she recalls crying in the shower every morning. "I guess I never got over it because I still feel ashamed." Anne said. Following that, Anne remembers feeling ashamed for the remainder of her childhood. As a straight "A" student she felt smart in school, but at home, her father would often criticize her for making mistakes with statements like, "Do you ever use your brain?"

Though Anne was a slender child, her father would often focus on her body and point to her behind and say, "You better watch it, you're getting chubby." Or, "Don't eat that, you'll be as big as your mom." When Anne started to run competitively, she remembers her dad taking an interest in her because he had been a competitive runner himself. She liked the attention at first, but the focus became negative quickly. After races, he would tell Anne that she had "no heart." Anne believes the race in Colorado was the beginning of her spiral downwards as a competitive runner. "I was never the same after that," she said. Demoralized, she lost an unhealthy amount of weight and had trouble sleeping at night. She trained with her father outside of team training and became so exhausted and emaciated, she could not continue to run. After a lot of thought, she decided to stop running and try out for the soccer team. She made the varsity team, and ecstatic to be unleashed from her father's focus, she happily played a sport he had nothing to do with. Unfortunately, the damage that was done to her self-esteem remained with her.

As Anne talked in therapy about the deep shame her father induced in her, she realized that she deserved none of it, and that it was actually shame her father had about himself. She carried her father's burden for him her entire life. She had protected him from feeling bad about himself and shouldered his weak self-esteem. Once she recognized and metabolized this in therapy, she was able to release herself. Unburdened by her father's baggage, she allowed herself to love and be loved, without shame or self-loathing. Anne finally allowed herself to be happy.

Chapter 9

THE RECIPIENT IN EVERYDAY LIFE

If the projective identification dynamic is present in the parent child relationship without the recipient aware, they are doomed to carry this pattern into their future relationships. Human beings are naturally attracted to the familiar, and because of this the recipient feels immediate chemistry with a projector. Being reminded of familial relationships, they then enter friendship and/or courtships with a new projector. In everyday interactions, a recipient can fall into their role almost automatically. Overly friendly and accommodating, they wonder why they are a continual target amongst groups of friends, at work, or even in routine interactions. If they encounter people who are *not* projectors, the recipients remain warm, friendly, and have healthy interactions. However, the world is full of projectors and therefore the recipient is constantly at risk.

Elane's daughter was a healthy, independent, beautiful five year old who was experiencing mild separation anxiety the second week of kindergarten. Elane felt a great deal of empathy for her daughter. She attempted to support her by talking her through the transition, giving her reassurance and encouragement and even making time to drop and pick her up from school rather than riding the bus. The teacher, a projector, seemed to blame Elane for her daughter's difficulty separating. She sent emails to Elane stating that this was unusual behavior and that Elane needed to get her daughter back on the bus. She also recommended Elane involve her in more play dates outside of Elane's home in to help her separate from Elane. In one email, the teacher stated, "I think its best you do not go on the field trip with us because your daughter is much stronger without you around." Elane was confused. She thought that mild separation anxiety was probably common for most kids starting all day kindergarten. In addition, her daughter's tears stopped within minutes of entering her classroom, and she functioned happily for the remainder of her day in school. An independent child, she had participated in play dates outside of the house for years, in addition to attending all day camps the previous summer and several sleepovers at other kid's houses. Independence was not an issue for her daughter.

Elane disclosed her conflicted feelings in session. She was reminded of the possibility that the teacher may be a projector, and as a recipient, Elane was vulnerable. She decided to send a firm, but polite email to the teacher, asserting that mild separation anxiety was a normal issue for kids starting kindergarten and that her child was extremely well adjusted and independent. Elane respectfully disagreed with the teacher's suggestion that she should refrain from chaperoning her daughter's field trip the following month because Elane was confident this issue would be resolved within a few days. The day after Elane sent the email, her daughter showed no signs of separation anxiety. She happily marched down the hall to her classroom. The teacher seemed refrain from blaming Elane, and seemed to be more respectful. Elane successfully stopped the projective identification in a positive manner. She politely, stood up for herself without becoming defensive, and corrected the teacher in a competent and professional manner. It is also interesting to consider how simultaneous the arrest of the projective identification was to the disappearance of her child's separation anxiety. Is it possible that a child who is neither a recipient nor a projector can sense when a projection is occurring with their mother, who is a recipient?

Another patient, Lynn, who worked for UPS, exemplifies the danger of everyday interactions for a recipient. She primarily worked out of her truck, and did not have a lot of interaction with co-workers. A friendly and cheerful person, and when given the opportunity Lynn readily engaged the employees of the businesses on her route in casual chit chat as she was completing her work. She had established friendly rapports with just about everybody on her route.

Lynn experienced a very difficult session with the therapist she was seeing at the time. A few days later, she was still experiencing "raw" emotions over the session. During her route, she proceeded to make a drop at a local psychiatrist's office. Though this was not her personal therapist, she had come to know the staff in this particular office very well over the years. She decided to disclose information about her recent session to a counselor with whom she was used to chatting. She asked the counselor if her emotional state was normal, to which counselor replied, "I don't know, but you have a low self-esteem and are probably being over sensitive," and abruptly walked away. Lynn described feeling humiliated and embarrassed. She blamed herself for the rupture in her therapy and regretted asking someone whom she thought had expertise in this area for their advice.

Chapter 10

BREAKING THE PATTERN

UNLEASHING THE INNER ROAR

Recognizing that you or someone you may be close to is possibly a recipient is the first step in ending the pattern. Keep in mind someone who may be vulnerable to other people's projections, and even identifying the projectors in your life. These people may come in the form of a spouse, sibling, mother-in- law, friend, colleague, neighbor, etc. If you are indeed a recipient, chances are good that you have acquired quite a few projectors. Gathered in the previous chapters, it is emotional distance that helps extinguish a projective identification relationship. Giving consideration to this fact, it is necessary to ponder the possibility of ending a marriage or a romantic relationship if you feel it involves this destructive dynamic. It is impossible to be emotionally close to a projector without damage to your self-esteem and dignity. If children are involved, this type of relationship can be extremely damaging to their psychological development and emotional well-being as they grow up baring witness to these accounts.

Relationships outside of marriages, however, are easier to deal with and do may not require severing the relationship. Salvaging these relationships while ending a painful projective identification cycle is possible, and not only frees the recipient from drama and pain but fosters a healthier relationship in which both parties benefit. Establishing safe emotional distance may sound simple, but there are a few critical changes must be made by the recipient. As described earlier, recipients participate in several behaviors that help maintain a destructive projective identification dynamic. The first behavior is allowing the projector in. The recipient believes they are less competent then the projector, so they approach the projector for advice or help. In doing so, they allow the projector access to their personal struggles. This gives the projector ammunition to distort this information and attack the recipient either in future interactions or behind the recipient's back, in order to uproot the recipient's reputation. Avoiding divulging important personal information keeps the projector at a safe distance. An additional tactic to create and maintain emotional distance with the projector is to decrease communication with them. Instead of talking on the phone, emailing or texting several times a week, limit the contact to once a week or once every other week. In order to disguise your attempt to create space in the relationship, always respond to their contact cordially. Avoid an interaction by letting them know you are glad they called, but you need to call them back later in the week when you have a break.

Due to the projective identification dynamic, the recipient feels like the projector is more competent in areas than they are, so they feel like they need the projector in order to be okay. For example, a recipient might have a friend (projector) who is the captain of their soccer team. The recipient is flattered and excited to be on the team but feels less capable on the field then the captain, so they attempt to stay in the projector's good graces in order to solidify their spot on the team. As terrifying as it is, the recipient has to muster up enough self-esteem to rely on their own merit instead of depending on a projector to maintain them in their position.

The recipient's continual tendency to stroke the projector's ego must also cease. This can be difficult because the recipient has become accustomed to complimenting the projector in order to keep the projector happy. In moments of insecurity, the recipient will often resort to fluffing the projector's ego in order to prevent the projector from criticizing or attacking them. This is a habit which perpetuates the cycle. If the recipient has enough confidence, they can refrain from nonsense and relate to people honestly, confidently, and directly, rather than "kissing up" in order to ensure people like them.

When the projector feels the hold on the recipient slipping because of the emotional distance the recipient has created, they may become aggravated. Initially, they will be charming and nice, perhaps inviting the recipient to spend time with them. However, if the recipient declines because they are attempting to emotionally distance themselves from the projector, the projector may become increasingly exasperated. It is at these times that the bullying behavior begin. The projector will begin to talk negatively about the recipient behind their back in an attempt to align people against the recipient. Mature healthy adults usually see through this kind of manipulation, but some do not. The people who align with the projector against the recipient, even though they realize the projector is distorting the truth, are the types of personalities that are insecure and tend to feel better about themselves if they can pick on someone else. Projectors are not only profoundly insecure, but they are actually intensely envious of the recipient. Recipients, because of their low self-esteem, are clueless as to why anyone would be jealous of them, so they do not consider that as a possibility. To a recipient, the only possibility is that they, themselves, are unworthy.

he hope is that with the recipient's subtle and diplomatic attempts to create emotional distance from the projector, they will land in a safe place out of the projector's reach. This allows them to be friendly and caring, but without making themselves vulnerable or available to the projector to mistreat. If recipients do not figure out a way to avoid projectors, or create emotional distance when they become involved with one, they may be bullied to the point of withdrawing socially. They lose faith in the existence of trustworthy people and give up on friendships. If they do begin to identify and deal with the projectors in a healthy manner, they have a better chance of surrounding themselves with non-projectors. For a recipient, a life free from projective identification allows them to maximize the talents and qualities that they had previously been too unconfident to explore.

The recipient's unrealized talents and qualities become a battle cry. Although the recipient will always be vulnerable to the dynamic of projective identification due to their childhood experiences, they will utilize ways to avoid or escape it. This allows them to feel confident and capable outside of the dynamic. Feeling confident allows them to take a chance on themselves. The women who comprised the support group described earlier are examples of a "recipient's roar". All successful, attractive, articulate, and intelligent women, they were excited and energized about their futures and the opportunities they were going to seize now that they were uninhibited by the projective identification dynamic. In each other's company, they were able to acknowledge the ridiculousness of what they have been taught to believe about themselves. Their empathy for one another and their shared belief that they did not deserve to be mistreated the way they had been, made them unusually strong. Free from emotional terrorism, their continued success and happiness seemed inevitable.

Chapter 11

HOW TO HANDLE

GROUP PROJECTIVE IDENTIFICATION

The group projective identification dynamic is very powerful. As explained in the first chapter, it is adult bullying at its best, beginning with a projector, who is extremely jealous of another person. This person becomes the projector's recipient. The projector finds something they deem unacceptable about their target and begins the process of group projective identification by dramatizing and distorting the truth about the recipient. Utilizing degrading and hateful language, they gossip about the recipient to anyone who will listen. As others align with the projector and participate in broadcasting the mistruths and distortions, the projector feels increasingly justified in their cause.

The recipient in this scenario is blindsided. The projector, who was once a friend or someone who the recipient trusted, has turned on them and is viciously attempting to align their mutual acquaintances against them. Recipient's become aware that their acquaintances view them as a deplorable human being and they now have to endure this. In the cases they have enough non-projectors in their life to cancel out the projectors, the risk for social alienation is extinguished, but chances are that as a recipient they have attracted a slew of projectors which now are sealing their fate.

For Elane, the group projection was so powerful, that gossip about her divorce seemed to spread to everyone in her small town. Mass emails were sent to groups of people outrageously distorting the details of their divorce. She was asked to leave her tennis team, and all of her new neighbors reported they had been approached by Elane's old friends in order talk negatively about her. People seemed to shun her everywhere she went. The dynamic was so powerful, that she began to have panic attacks after encountering these projectors. She had a difficult time participating in the activities she used to enjoy because she was continually exposed to people who condemned her.

The entire "witch hunt", was a phenomenon Elane could not wrap her head around. She could not understand how people could side with someone who was obviously abusive and malicious. The tendency for people to join a projector is fascinating because projectors are insecure, mean spirited bullies. Unfortunately, it is people who are also insecure and jealous of others that perpetuate the projector's agenda by participating in the bullying. The recipient becomes unable to defend themselves knowing their confrontation will not only cause additional drama with the projectors, but will also give the projectors new material to distort and use against them. They become accepting of the feeling that people hate them. This is tortuous for a recipient who spends a great deal of energy attempting to ensure people like them. While they are tolerating this uncomfortable feeling, however, they can fight back in a different way that allows them to win against the projectors.

Group projectors spend a lot of time gossiping and spreading hate, so they don't have much time for anything else. Recipients do. Recipients can take this time to expand their career, take on a new endeavor, write a book, invent something, run a marathon, take their kids to the Grand Canyon, rescue a dog, volunteer at a homeless shelter, go back to school, etc. Instead of allowing these projectors to dismantle their lives, they need to invest in it. Usually smart with creative tendencies, recipients can use the anger they feel towards the projector as energy to do great things that not only enhance their success as an individual, but infuse the world with good.

Recipients, unlike projectors, have a shot at being happy. Their happiness is derived from the satisfaction they get from helping and being with others. They find joy in other people's happiness and sorrow in other people's pain. Able to connect and resonate with other people's experiences, they have the ability to empathize and share in a way that allows them to be close with other people. Also, because they have been devalued, they resonate with people who are degraded, marginalized, and bullied. The first person to defend someone who is being stripped of their dignity, is usually a recipient. Recipients are often humanitarians.

If the recipient can tolerate the group projective identification, while remaining strong enough to love, receive love from their children, family and friends, they will survive the storm. Their survival will eventually prevent the projectors from bullying them again. Taking the high road and staying above the projector's fray, creates emotional distance and will stop the group projective identification dynamic. The projector's goal is to destroy the recipient's reputation in their community. They become frustrated when the recipient seems unfazed, and continues to achieve personal and professional success. It may take a few months, but like all bullies, if they are not successfully terrorizing their victims they lose interest.

CHECKLIST

For Stopping Projective Identification- Bullying

1. **Create emotional distance:**

   Creating emotional distance is most effective with projective identifications which   occur in friendships and extended familial relationships in which the projectors most prominent tactic is to talk
   negatively behind your back, distorting the truth to mutual friends
   and acquaintances with the goal of aligning people against you.

   A) Discontinue involving the projector in your life. Refrain from asking
   for their help with anything and avoid disclosing anything personal.

   B) Quantifiably decrease communication. Stop texting, emailing or
   calling the projector, and when responding to their texts or calls, be
   polite and cheerful, but short and concise. Let them know you will
   call them when things get less busy for you.

   C) Avoid getting sucked into their dramatic scenarios.

   D) Resurrect healthy boundaries. Do not appease, join in, or pla-
   cate the projector by doing favors or helping them out.

   E) Hold your head up high in the presence of the projector. Without telling them, show them you are unshaken by their antics and
   you are confident in yourself.

2. **Stand up to the projector politely and assertively:**

   This method should only be used if the projector continually blames
   you or picks on you face to face, or if they attack you directly
   through email or texts.

A) Respond unemotionally and without attacking back.

B) Without the use of dramatic language, acknowledge the incorrectness and in appropriateness of the projectors attack.

C) Politely tell them to stop.

D) When they become incensed and enraged at you, they will attempt to push your buttons. Do not react. Politely excuse yourself from the conversation.

E) They will continue to talk negatively behind you back, but ignore, ignore, ignore. Hopefully, they will tire themselves out and people will get sick of hearing it.

3. **Outsmart projector/bully:**

Most effective approach in marriages or bullying scenarios when the projector has control or leverage over the recipient.

A) Use wit and intellect to use the projectors own narcissism against them.

Example 1: Jan's husband verbally and emotionally abused his children, but planned on fighting for custody for the children in order to hurt Jan, who had been the primary caretaker for the children during the marriage. Jan knew her husband had a very short temper and hated to be disturbed by the kids after work or on the weekends. Although it was difficult, she left them with him a few times. He quickly came unglued with the children and threw fits of rage. After a few days, he yelled in front of them, "These kids have no respect for me!" "You can have them!" Jan was granted full physical custody of the children.

Example 2: Dons x-wife was extremely controlling. She needed to know every detail about his life. She insisted that Don purchase a house phone at his new place so she could talk to their kids when they were with him. Yet, Don knew this was her way of finding out whether he was home or not, as well as, monopolizing the kids during Don's visit because she assumed they would pick up whenever she called. So, Don installed a house phone, but turned the ringer off. After 15 unanswered calls to his house one night, she gave up on that phone.

4. **Pass the bully up in life:**

Most effective in every projective Identification or bullying scenario.

A) Invest in your life by applying for a promotion, running a marathon, planting a garden, writing a book, going back to school… paint, sculpt, go to a conference, etc.

B) Believe in yourself. There are many things the projector made you believe you are terrible at. Reclaim these things and learn to be good at them. Initially, it may be difficult without confidence, but try and try and try until you are successful.

C) Give back by spending time with people who don't have anyone. Help the disadvantaged in any way you can.

D) Love your children with reckless abandon.

Chapter 12

KINDNESS, RESPECT AND LOVE
FIND THE RECIPIENT

After years of being devalued and degraded, it is normal for the recipient to begin strongly disliking the projector. However, they deny or disguise their dislike for the projector because they still believe they either need the projector or feel indebted to this person. Yet, because they are capable of emotional growth, they slowly and methodically become aware that they are being manipulated and mistreated. When this awareness grows, they begin to explore the possibility of freeing themselves from the projector. Often the light bulb moment occurs when they meet someone who treats them with kindness and respect. If this person happens to come in the form of a romantic partner, the recipient begins to open their eyes. Realizing that another human being wants to talk to them like an equal, is interested in what they think, values their opinion, and cares about them in a genuine way, might tip the scale for the recipient. After years of being emotionally isolated, lonely, and disrespected, finding someone who makes them feel valued and loved is much like being born again.

There is a strong possibility that projectors may be lousy lovers. Inherently selfish and in need of treating the recipient in a demeaning manner, they are many times mechanical, self-serving, and uncaring in bed. Chances are also strong with the implication that they are only concerned about their own "satisfaction".

Most of the recipients treated in therapy, report they avoid sex with their partners. Elane had reported she conceded to sex due to the guilt her partner would inflict on her if she didn't agree, and when in bed she closed her eyes and gritted her teeth until the interaction was over. Ann, was nicknamed the ice queen by her partner because of her aversion to sex with him. Both women thought there was something wrong with them. Elane contemplated the possibility that she was gay, and Ann went to the doctor to get estrogen shots because of the extreme lack of desire she felt for her husband. Yet, when they encountered men who demonstrated genuine love and respect for them, they came alive. They both felt desire so strong, they described it as feeding a starving baby. They felt physical sensations they had never felt before and did not think were possible. Giddy with delight, they realized what they had been missing for years and years. The first light bulb may have been intellectual, but the second was sensual. The joy expressed on these women's faces was palpable. Being loved and cherished was a feeling they had not felt in years.

Chapter 13

I'D RATHER BE HIT

The powerful and fascinating aspect about the projective identification dynamic is the unconscious transfer that occurs. It is more than a spraying of hurtful words resulting in the recipient's disempowerment. A verbal exchange does not necessarily have to occur for the dynamic to work. Projectors inflict unconsciously inflict damage, making the invisible warfare is nearly impossible to identify and diagnose if the recipient is uneducated about this type of dynamic. Both verbal and physical abuse are proof of a pathological partner, yet many projectors are smart enough to do the damage without resorting to physical or verbal means.

Elane had recently been awarded a prestige's grant for her research, which included a monetary advance to account for her salary. She was intensely proud of herself and thought of it as the crowning achievement of her career. She told several close friends and her children. One day, at her son's basketball game, still glowing from the news, she encountered her projector and immediately felt insignificant. She described feeling like a silly little girl with a dumb idea that would never amount to anything.

Demoralized and deflated she came to her session sad and uninspired about the topic she had been passionate about for years. However, she was aware as to why she felt this way. She explained that her projector had sabotaged most of the joyful occasions in her life. He couldn't tolerate watching her enjoy her kids or anyone else. He would interject himself into the interaction and tease her in a malicious and degrading manner. She remembered saying to him at one point, "You find a way to ruin everything good that happens to me." Whether it was having a good time with friends, her children, or feeling good about an accomplishment, her husband would devalue Elane with malicious comments he excused as "joking around." This experience had occurred so frequently, that Elane felt it automatically in his presence. Though Elane's husband would occasionally verbalize supportive comments, she realized it was impossible for him to be genuinely being happy for her. She eventually realized that actions spoke louder than words.

The continual experience of her partner sabotaging the joy in her life, further intensified the non-verbal projective identification dynamic. Her awareness that his intent was to destroy her confidence and ruin her relationships made her feel like a human target waiting to be fired upon. Whether he used words, glares, or backstabbing manipulations as his weapons, she felt the potential onslaught deep in her unconscious. The projector's true intent is to destroy the recipient, and that is what is communicated often without words. This type of psychological assault is so destructive that it can be more intense than physical pain. In fact, in group therapy, nearly all of members wished their projectors had struck them physically. Although they described feeling victimized and mistreated by their projector, they believed it was "In their heads" because the mistreatment was not tangible. They truly believed that if their projector had hit them, they would have left the projector instead of blaming themselves and continuing to exist in the dysfunctional relationship.

Carrie provides another example of the projector's ability to disarm a recipient's self-esteem with just their presence. Her situation occurred when she had to drop off, and pick up her kids after visits with their dad. Initially, her projector was verbally abusive to her. After involving her attorney, he remained silent for some of the exchanges. The silence was sometimes worse than his verbal onslaught. She would leave the exchange shaken and anxious, insecure in her ability to support her children. Although she had established a thriving practice which was growing every day, she felt incompetent. In session, she said this feeling stayed with her for days. Her friends who were aware of her accomplishments could tell when she had been in the presence of her ex, because she lost her confidence. Attempting anything to help their friend return to normal, they would send her empowering quotes, messages and lyrics from popular songs. Carrie realized she changed when she was in the presence of her projector and began to actively seek support from her friends and family after the exposure.

Jan kept two quotes with her at all times, and read them several times a day when she started to feel insecure. The first quote is entitled, "You Didn't Lover Her," from the TV show Greys Anatomy:

You Didn't Love Her

"You just didn't want to be alone. Or maybe, she was good for your ego. Or maybe she made you feel better about your miserable life, but you didn't love her. Because you don't destroy people you love."

Untitled

"I believe that we are who we choose to be. Nobody is going to come and save you. You've got to save yourself. Nobody is going to give you anything. You've got to go out and fight for it. Nobody knows what you want except you, and nobody will be as sorry as you if you don't get it. So don't give up on your dreams."

Carrie's friends rallied around her after an exposure with her projector. One friend nicknamed it the projective identification syndrome, or PIS. Carrie would call him up stating, "I'm not myself today, and I got "PIS-ed" last night." Her friends would text her and her empowering messages. Eventually, they took the sting out of her situation by making "got PIS-ed" into a joke and a catch phrase for their group of friends.

After the recipient has created emotional distance with the projector, they will still have tender spots. They entered the relationship with insecurities which were poked at over and over until the weakness became a gaping detriment. Instead of supporting and encouraging the recipient with tasks related to their insecurities, the projector shamed and deemed them hopeless in these categories. As a result, the recipient gave up these activities assuming that their incompetence was too insurmountable. When independence from the projector occurs, the open wound begins to heal but is still a source of extreme vulnerability for the recipient. Only time and perseverance with activities related to their insecurities will help. As the old adage says "Rome wasn't built in a day." Nor is a solid self-esteem. The chances are exponentially greater in building a strong foundation if the projector is not involved.

Elane felt extreme insecurities even after her projector had left the picture. She paid her credit card balance off every month, and still beat herself up for purchases she put on the card. Even a small purchase was rifled with guilt and stress. The enjoyment of shopping flew out the window. Every check out register gave her a stomach ache; her projector's voice replaying in her head, "You will never make it financially. You're a train wreck with money." She knew it would be an uphill battle, but her lack of faith in her abilities made it an even more painful one. With support, she acknowledged her insecurities and kept going. Eventually, her deep insecurities turned into careful consideration and the satisfaction she derived from spending her own money was priceless.

Carrie's personal therapy was jogging outside. Slightly overweight, she was told by her projector that she was unfit to run a marathon. After her divorce, she hit the road harder than ever. On race day she felt strong, but at the thirteen mile marker, her muscles atrophied and cramps gripped her side. She was beat. "He was right," she said to herself." Yet, the cheers of the bystanders changed her mind. She fought through the negativity and finished the race with a mile split faster than when she started. She crossed the finish line with a smile on her face.

Even after a projector is gone, the projection lingers until time and success drum it out. It will not happen overnight. Like everything else, it takes time, trial and error, practice, learning lessons, and forgiving yourself, so you can try again. It is a struggle.

Be your own hero. And your daughter's. And your son's. You can do it!

Techniques for Quieting Anxiety and Combating Hopelessness

1. **Participate in a physical activity that connects the mind and body in a soothing and meditative way.**

    A) Yoga

    B) Running

    C) Walking

    D) Massage Therapy

2. **Engage in something spiritual**

    A) Go to church, mass, synagogue, chapel, etc.

    B) Pray

3. **Spend time with the old or the young**

    A) Do something fun with your kids or your nieces, nephews, etc.

    B) Spend time with your parents or grandparents

4. **Journal**

5. **Listen to empowering music**

6. **Cook for someone special**

7. Read empowering material

8. Go to therapy

9. Volunteer

10. Spend time with your pet

11. Consider medication

12. Take a friend to a funny movie

Chapter 14

DELUSIONAL AMNESIA

Projectors are not be able to accept that the recipient is gone, even after the divorce is final. They not only distort the truth about the recipient, but also distort reality in order to protect their self-esteem. The projector has their own view of reality, and conveniently forget their wrongdoings. It's a form of delusional amnesia. Even when the recipient, who can point out the exact date and time of an incident and even describes it in detail for the projector, he/she denies this reality and erases it from their memory. They do not remember participating in the terrible things they have done.

In group, Sally described her husband as a "pathological liar" because he denied the horrible things he had done, which she could recount in detail. Yet, he was so adamant about his own reality which was so different from the truth, the only explanation to Sally seemed was that he was a liar. Elane's husband was similar. He played the innocent role with such authenticity that he was able to convince all of their mutual friends that he was the perfect husband instead of an abusive one.

This became clear to Elane one night when her husband showed up at her house in an attempt to convince her to stay married to him. Elane recounted for him in detail the dozens of awful and abusive things he had done. As she was talking he appeared to be listening, but the following day, these occurrences were apparently wiped clean from his memory as he continued to bully her. It was as if the incidents she had identified for him the night before had evaporated in his brain overnight. Jan's case offers another example of this; she and her husband attended couples therapy. Her husband became angry during one session and began shaking his finger in Jan's face, calling her a "terrible mother" and a "disgusting person." After attempting to settle him down, Jan had a chance to talk. She disclosed that the night before, her husband had taken seven Zanex and tried to strangle her. In response, he blew up and blamed her for his rage, without realizing it, he had inadvertently admitted to the incident. A few days later, Jan came to session and reported that he had emphatically denied the incident to his attorney and hers. The next day, he became enraged and threw a cup of coffee at Jan. Again, he denied the occurrence.

In the beginning of the relationship, the projector's ability to erase their abusive actions from their mind is profound, which causes the recipient to doubt their own recollections. Traumatic incidents are burned into the victim's memory, as is true with most trauma, and these memories are overwhelmingly painful. For the recipient, it is easier to try to forget the experiences than accept the reality of the abusive situation. They surrender to the projector's reality because theirs is too painful. This is a temporary fix to a permanent problem. Eventually, the recipient must come to terms with their memories and honor them. By honoring their memory, they honor themselves.

Jan's traumatic experience exemplifies this. At group, she retold the story of her husband losing control, overdosing on his medication and attempting to strangle her. The group members were empathic, but asked her why she did not call the police. Jan stated that she was "in shock." By the time she realized the gravity of the situation, she felt it was too late to call the police, but she solemnly promised to call 911 immediately if the situation became physical again.

Due to the distorted version of a projector's reality, they have a difficult time accepting the truth that the recipient is not under their control anymore. Functioning in denial, the projector seizes any and every opportunity to interact with the recipient in order to assert some sort of control over them. After nearly a year of divorce proceedings, Carrie's husband told their children that he was moving to Carrie's neighborhood just one block away, and that he and Carrie were getting back together. Ideally, by this point, a recipient should become savvy enough to assert strong boundaries with the projector in order to ensure emotional distance.

Adding fuel to the fire, when the projector discovers that the recipient has a love interest, they quickly reinstate the projective Identification. Instead of attacking just the recipient, they wage war on the recipient's new partner and their relationship. Unfortunately because the projector knows the recipients weaknesses intimately, and has been exploiting them for years, they have an advantage. With the recipient having had subjected themselves to the projective identification dynamic for years, it will take at least a few months of emotional distance in order to become free. Most recipients are fairly insecure about their ability to function in a relationship because they have been blamed for problems in their prior relationships. The projector uses this vulnerability to their advantage and attacks the recipient's selection attempting to devalue their new partner. Often, he will attempt to plant doubt in the recipient's mind about the character of her new partner, accusing him of being a terrible person.

Another tactic the projector uses, is that he has "knowledge" about the new partner. Elane's case, her projector accused her new partner of being a cheater, womanizer and user. Although Elane knew these things were not true, she began to doubt herself and her partner. Elane's projector would also refer to him as a "loser" because he didn't make as high of a salary as he did. Using racial slurs, he also attacked her new partner's children. Although Elane vehemently disagreed with the projector's statements, he was able to make her doubt herself enough to temporarily take the joy out of her relationship for a while. It was as if he had shown the projective identification spotlight onto her partner, and was able to effect Elane's feelings about him just as he was able to effect Elane's feelings about herself. Fortunately, Elane was able to hold onto the relationship until she could gain enough distance from the projective identification dynamic to disarm it.

Chapter 15

EDDIE: A MALE RECIPIENT'S ACCOUNT

Eddie, a pharmaceutical representative, was well dressed and articulate. Yet, there was a profound sadness about him. He explained he was attending the appointment in place of his daughter, Haley, whom he thought desperately needed to be in therapy. As a divorced father he felt estranged from his daughter because of her volatile relationship with his new fiancé, Gloria. Because he lived with Gloria, the visits with Haley took place at her home which created a great deal of tension between the ladies. Gloria made efforts to involve Haley in the household activities along with her and her own daughter, but Haley refused to participate. Haley frequently locked herself in the bathroom or bedroom with her phone and spent the evenings alone. Gloria, irate at Haley's response, deemed her to be disrespectful. Eddie made every attempt to coax and persuade Haley to come out, but with no success. Haley perceived Gloria as controlling and aloof. During another visit, Eddie and Gloria took the girls out to breakfast where Haley began to text at the table. Eddie politely asked her to put her phone away, however Haley remained silent and continued to text. Gloria, who was becoming irritated with the situation and reprimanded Haley. Haley got up from the table, and went outside to call her mom. Her mom took her home and Eddie and Gloria were unable to see Haley for the remainder of the weekend.

Eddie explained that his marriage to Haley's mom had been dysfunctional. After the divorce, he attempted to support both his ex-wife and Haley by taking care of Haley at her mom's house every weekday night while his ex-wife went to work. He reported he enjoyed bringing Haley dinner and loved helping her with her homework. In addition, Eddie supported Haley's participation in volleyball. He attended most of her games and took her to all of her out of state tournaments. Although this caused some minor hardships for Eddie because it required him to leave work early as well as neglect his own home and personal life, he enjoyed supporting his daughter. Eddie empathized with his ex-wife's need to schedule appointments in the evening and understood her desire to maintain an active social and dating life, so he gladly filled in. After about six years, Eddie met Gloria, and thought it might be okay to date. He disclosed feeling guilty, initially, but he believed enough time had elapsed for Haley to have recovered from the divorce and to be at peace with him having a girlfriend. In session, he admitted that he felt responsible for Haley's "acting out" behaviors. He asked if he should end his relationship with Gloria, but eventually decided that if he followed through with Gloria's suggestion to try and incorporate several different parenting interventions and behavior modifications things might work out.

A few weeks later, Eddie described looking forward to getting away with Gloria for a long weekend. He was aware that Haley might have a national tournament that weekend depending on her performance at state, but he persuaded Haley's mom to take her if her team advanced. Eddie felt conflicted about missing Haley's biggest competition, but was aware that the weekend with Gloria was very important

Distraught, panicked, and depressed, Eddie attended the next session and told me "he had made a huge mistake." Haley qualified for the national competition, but her mom changed her mind and announced she could not take her. Although Eddie pleaded with her to reconsider, Haley's mom would not. He insisted the situation was his fault because he was "conflict avoidant" and wasn't assertive enough with his ex-wife. When he told Gloria about the conflict, she became angry and decided "to put her foot down." She said if Eddie cancelled their trip, she would not allow him to have his weekend visits with Haley at her home in the future. Eddie was devastated. He believed he had to forgo Haley's tournament if he wanted to salvage his relationship with Gloria. He berated himself for the situation and was emphatic in his belief that

Gloria was justified in her demand that he fulfill his commitment to her.

After a great deal of discussion, Eddie realized that a healthy relationship should rarely require one party levying an ultimatum, especially if the ultimatum involved a child. He realized that although Gloria had many degrees and appeared intellectual, her assertions were nothing more than threats. He decided that if his partner truly loved and cared for him, she would not purposefully come in between he and his daughter, no matter how difficult the dynamic. Eddie started to realize that he might be sandwiched in between two projectors and geared up for a battle. Protecting and preserving his relationship with his daughter became a priority.

The discovery that Haley was ranked first in her junior class at a competitive private high school came by surprise. Well-liked by her peers and described as "kind," was the opinion stumbled upon unintentionally. These were important aspects of Haley's life that were omitted by Eddie and Gloria. At the acknowledgement of his daughter's extreme success, on and off the court, and the affirmation that he must have done a great job helping Haley with her homework for many years, Eddie was dumbfounded. The realization that his daughter was a child to be proud of instead of ashamed of, as Gloria had insisted, was a new idea to him. The proposition that he had contributed to her success was something he had never considered.

It is important to consider the possibility of the projective identification aspect as it pertains to many different relationships. Eddie's case is not rare, and in fact many men are recipients. Men and women are quite different in how they process emotions, and while women seem to be more generally accepted when they long to remedy their "victim" status, men are often times ridiculed. We find that men have a more difficult time accepting being recipients, and perhaps feel a sense of fear and embarrassment tackling the issue head on. Having to deal with the issue means it actually does exist, and for some men this is a jab at their ego.

Chapter 16

BULLYING

Despite the anti-bullying campaigns within school systems, bullying seems to be more prevalent than ever. This cruel trend begins at a very young age and effects thousands of children every day. Suzie, an eight year old described being persistently bullied. In Suzie's class, each day students were to read a paragraph out loud from their reading book. After their paragraph was finished, they would select the next student to read. Suzie said that every day that year, except for one, she had been picked last. The day she had not been picked last, she was picked second to last, which made her feel happy. Suzie attributed this to her broken arm and new cast, which all of her classmates seemed interested in. Yet, her position as the last reader resumed the following day. She also described incidents when she would select a seat and everybody around her would get up and move to seats across the room.

One day, the girl she identified as the most ruthless, Yasmine, had referred to Suzie as a, "fat loser." Later on the playground, the Boys taunted each other with, "you're going to marry Suzie," and the rest of the boys would pretend to throw up. The constant bullying dismantled her self-esteem. She became terrified to fall asleep at night, and she cried and clung to her mom before going to school.

Her father attended a therapy session and when it was described to him as to what had been occurring in Suzie's classroom, he began to tear up. The agony he felt at the thought of his daughter experiencing such cruelty on a daily basis was overwhelming. He and his wife were aware that Suzie had been bullied, and they had met with the teacher to try and stop it, but they were not aware that it had been continuing and intensifying. In session, he repeated a conversation he had with Suzie while getting ready for bed the night before. Suzie asked him why she was the one being picked on at school. Why didn't the other kids get picked on? Why was she the one? His heart broke for her and he wasn't sure how to respond, but he reassured her that it wasn't because there was something wrong with her. The only explanation he could think of was that she might be in a situation one day to help someone else who was being bullied. Unlike her classmates who join the bullying, she might be the person to take a stand and stop it because she knows how it feels. Unfortunately, Suzie didn't seem reassured, so he stayed with her, hugging her until she fell asleep.

The following week, Suzie's parents excitedly disclosed in therapy that a meeting had been initiated by the school with the parents of Yasmine. They reported that although the meeting had occurred two days before, Suzie had declined to talk about how things were going with Yasmine, but they were confident Suzie would discuss it in therapy. During the session Suzie seemed sad, however, attempts to break the ice with her were successful with the use of card game. After a few minutes, she began discussing how things were going for her in school. She said, "My principal had a meeting with Yasmine. I thought things would be better, but it only made her meaner. She even got the only friend I had at school to be mean to me. Yasmine is best friends with her now." As her therapist, I empathized with how hurt and disappointed she must be and made sure she knew she did not deserve such treatment.

A few weeks later, Suzie came to session visibly excited. She brought in an award she had received at an all school assembly. After enjoying the lots of praise she said: "It was really fun to get an award, but guess who got the kindness award?" "Yasmine." How could happen? Suzie was dumbfounded, but from a therapeutic perspective this indicated that Yasmine was very careful to exhibit her "meanness" outside of adult supervision. Unlike children, adults have the luxury to leave situations. They can leave jobs, friendships, and marriages if they feel they are being bullied, but kids cannot. They must go to school. There is no escape and they are usually alone in their plight. Many kids are so humiliated by the bullying that they can't bear to tell their parents because they are embarrassed, so the torture continues.

Tina, fourteen, attended therapy for about a year. She was mildly depressed, but seemed to be doing well with antidepressants and weekly counseling, however, one day she attended session and tearfully disclosed that her friends had "turned" on her. She said they sent her negative messages on Facebook and began to refer to her as "annoying" and "fake." At one point, they stopped her from sitting with them at lunch and started to shun her at school. The worst experience for Tina was when they told her to "Kill herself because the world would be a better place without her." Embarrassed and wanting the hostility to stop, Tina did not tell anyone. She worried that if she told her parents or teachers, she would re-ignite her friend's anger and they would become more vengeful. So, she tolerated the abuse, and began attempting to make new friends. She eventually was successful in separating from her original group of friends, but admitted to feeling suicidal several times during the thick of the bullying.

Although there are anti-bullying policies in almost every school, they often times do not seem to be effective. Teenagers commonly use technology to bully, but they also utilize social exclusion. Aligning their victim's friends against them, they exclude the adolescent from the group. Unlike cyber bullying where the offense can be reported, tracked, and the offender held accountable, there is no way for a parent or teacher to regulate kids from excluding one particular child from their social circle. The effects of this social exclusion are profound and sometimes life altering for a number of important developmental reasons. A teenager's friends are their world. Friendships are interwoven into almost every facet of an adolescent's life. If they are not spending time with friends, they are usually in their room texting or chatting with them online. A parent is lucky to reel them in once a week to share a meal or have a conversation with them. This is a normal phenomenon during the separation and individuation process when the young adult is attempting to establish their own identity and separate from their parents.

All adolescence work through the unstable process of formulating and solidifying their identity. This instability increases their vulnerability to the psychological effects of bullying. When they are ostracized from their peers, they have not only lost their friends, but feel they've lost their world. More importantly they have lost a sense of who they are. Their identity is derived from their peer relationships, and these relationships are interwoven into every aspect of the adolescents lives such as; activities, interests, hobbies and achievements. The fragility of an adolescent's identity and sense of self during the adolescent years is exemplified in the case of Gunner, a teenage boy who tragically took his own life. Several of Gunner's friends including his best friend, Sheila, came to therapy after his suicide. Unanimously, he was described as "having lots of friends," "happy go lucky" and "popular." No one saw signs of depression or anxiety. Sheila felt everybody loved Gunner and that he had a number of close friends. She said that all of their friends went to Gunner with their problems because he was a "good listener" and "very caring." When Sheila was upset, she said Gunner would drop everything to spend time with her and support her. "He cared more about his friends then he did himself," she stated. "He put his friends first."

Sheila's account states that the night that Gunner took his own life he was with a young woman who had the opposite personality type. Sheila described her as "insensitive" and "rude." Yet, according to his friends, Gunner had a crush on her. During the course of the evening, she and Gunner had been drinking alcohol and, by reports from Gunners friends, she had rejected him. Gunner became extremely depressed and emotional. He indicated to her that he felt suicidal, yet, she seemed unconcerned and left Gunner alone. Within a few minutes, he hung himself in his closet. There were multiple factors which contributed to this tragedy. Some things we will never know, however several suggest a projective identification might have been at play. Gunner might have been a recipient. He was the first to defend his friends when they were being picked on. He was sensitive, empathic, a people pleaser, and overly took responsibility for situations.

Gunner had texted several friends earlier that afternoon to see if they could get together. Coincidentally, most of his friends were busy which reportedly upset Gunner. It's possible he interpreted their unavailability as a sign that he had done something wrong in his relationships. Another factor was alcohol. He was under the influence, which may have intensified the negativity of his emotional and psychological state. The last factor would be his interaction with a possible projector. Not only did the young woman seem to reject Gunner rather callously, but her actions after his death support the probability that she was a projector.

After Gunner's death, the young woman involved seemed unfazed and unemotional regarding his suicide. At his funeral, Gunners parents asked the young woman to refrain from speaking, yet, she ignored their request and got up to speak about Gunner. Later that month, after posting several insensitive messages online about Gunner, Gunner's mom asked her to avoid including her sons name in her postings. The young lady retaliated rudely stating that she could do whatever she wanted to. She had no empathy for a mom who had just lost her child. She also exhibited an extreme lack of empathy the night Gunner took his own life. When he admitted to feeling suicidal, she did not try to comfort him or help him.

It may seem far-fetched to claim that projective identification was partly responsible for this loss of life, but, as explained earlier, a projector can effect a recipient's self-esteem so profoundly that they feel worthless and ashamed of who they are. It's a dark and hopeless place. If intoxication is added to the fragile identity of an adolescent, it can be lethal.

Helping a recipient Identify that they are a recipient can be proactive. It is not enough to simply label a kid with "low self-esteem," rather, talking about how they allow themselves to be devalued and taken advantage of in certain relationships may be helpful. One of the most intelligent things a teenager can do during their adolescent years is to diversify their friend groups. If one group of friends decides to bully or exclude them, they have other friend groups to be absorbed into.

Outside of cyber bullying, and social exclusion, there is the traditional "locker room" bullying. This occurs when there is a primary bully who degrades and humiliates a victim. Common advice in these situations has been to instruct the victim to stand up to the bully and even "punch them in the face". Yet, what people forget is that it is seldom a one to one ratio. A bully's first step in the process of bullying is to recruit others alongside him. So even if the victim is 350 pounds of solid muscle, he is no match for eight other co-bullies. Having a victim defend his or herself by using physical violence, can be a slippery slope. There have been situations when kids have been bullied so pervasively and systematically for years that they have a psychological breakdown. If kids are granted permission to use physical violence to defend themselves, why wouldn't it be ok, in their minds, to use a weapon? Being in the middle of a psychological breakdown, and advised to retaliate, is recipe for extreme violence such as gun violence. If violence is condoned, the floodgates are opened. If there is one thing we have learned through history, it's that violence perpetuates violence.

Standing up to a bully is key, however, doing it through the appropriate channels is often times ineffective. So, how does a victim stop the bullying? They must outsmart the bully who always has some hidden insecurities. These insecurities are the reason the bully targets their victims. This person is looking for an emotional reaction from their victim, usually hoping to scare or humiliate them. If the victim can avoid showing their emotions, they can effectively frazzle the bully. This is a prime time to point out to the bully, they are aware of the bully's need to pick on someone in order to feel good about themselves. Identifying the bully's motive is key. If the victim can clue in onto what the bully is insecure about, they may be able to further expose that person's weakness. Perhaps the bully is insecure about his athletic ability, physical structure, prowess with the opposite sex, intelligence, age, etc. The victim should figure this out and mention it to the bully.

Bullies are profoundly insecure, but compensate with arrogance and narcissism, they are partially blind having a version of reality that is distorted. This makes him vulnerable. If the victim can find a way to appear calm, unfazed, and utilize wit to put the bully on the defense, they have a chance. When a bully's intent to humiliate is reversed and he becomes the emotional one, the victim has successfully turned the tables. Hopefully, this will teach the bully not to bother the victim again. If the victim can pull this off calmly, confidently, assertively and with class, he will be successful.

Chapter 17

THE DOUBLE STANDARD

In the United States of America, we like to view racism, homophobia, and sexism as extinct. People have fought to make changes and room for the acceptance of people's differences. Women have fought for their right to vote, and won. Many other minority groups have worked hard to make big changes within the fabric of this country. However, we still see subtle and even more blatant forms of stereotyping and prejudice in modern day. Today, situations commonly occur of parents who claim they are not homophobic, yet deny their own adult children their right to sexuality. Women, who leave their dysfunctional marriages, are persecuted, and minorities are treated like they should feel privileged to live amongst the homogenous.

Different socioeconomic groups seem to have different views of the world from a diversity standpoint. Trends can be found in smaller middle-class areas where diversity is more widely accepted. Perhaps due to the common theme of hard work, and modest living that more securely ties the community together. While in some upper class Midwest American areas, there seems to be an elitist and narcissistic attitude. They have worked hard for their success, yet they some feel entitled to operate from a superior stance, which over time breeds insensitivity, intolerance, and the belief they are entitled to judge and persecute other human beings. In this culture, it is "social suicide" to leave your successful husband, even if he is emotionally abusive. Ironically, in these social circles it is acceptable for a husband to actively cheat on his wife. It is also socially acceptable for a husband to fondle, kiss, or sleep with another man's wife. In some cases, infidelity might even boost a man's social status. Divorce is considered admirable for a man because his wife is not making him happy and he is being honest with her about the demise of the relationship. The opposite is true for a woman. If a woman decides to divorce a wealthy husband, even if he is abusive, she will pay for it socially with a scarlet letter.

Another rather archaic view is the belief that couples should stay together for their children. There are thousands of children and adolescents in treatment for depressive disorders who come from intact families. Families with a traditional make up and a healthy income do not necessarily breed well-adjusted children. It requires healthy parents and a loving marriage to facilitate children with solid self-esteems, who can love instead of hate. If the marriage is an uncooperative and angry union, chances are the kids will suffer under this cloud of hostility. Dissolving the destructive partnership frees the children up from existing in a negative environment. A happy mom parenting under her own roof with confidence and love, and a dad who isn't allowed to humiliate mom anymore, or vice versa, is the most responsible and unselfish choice. If the pathological marriage continues, the children pay the price. Little girls grow up believing that degradation and disrespect are normal in a relationship, and little boys believe bullying another human being is their right. Human beings are made to love and be loved, with kindness and respect.

Chapter 18

HEROES, PLEASE STAND UP

ACCOUNTS OF REAL LIFE HEROES

The crime in the projective identification dynamic is that the cycle is continuous and pathological. Whether an adolescent is being bullied, a man or woman is being mistreated in a marriage, a person is continually humiliated at work, or a child is constantly degraded by their parent, it is unhealthy and needs to be stopped. The belief that a human being has the right to judge and condemn another human being for reasons they personally deem appropriate is narcissistic. In fact, it is against the core values of most religions. Yet, people participate in this evil cycle without a thought. Is it easier to "pick on" rather than "be picked on?" It is difficult to believe that, we as a human beings, are this weak. Is this the way we want to live as a society? With hate and emotional destruction as our motivator in daily life? Years go by, and still, the anti-bullying campaigns within the schools seem to constantly be ineffective.

Even the "popular kids" admit that bullying is rampant. Jackie, an adolescent stated, "The bullying is so bad and it happens every day, every second at school." When asked why it was happening, she said, "We learn it from our parents." She described walking out of school with her mother who commented on a classmate of hers. Her mom stated, "She barely has any clothes on. She looks like a slut." Jackie turned to her mom and said, "Mom! You have no idea what that girl's story is. She has had a very tough life." Another child, Sheila, stated, "You cannot walk down the hall without seeing four kids humiliating and demoralizing one." She continued with, "we have those anti-bullying rallies and speakers, and for a day people are nice, but then the bullies go right back to their cruel ways."

Outside of the bullying/projective identification cycle, the strength and character of ordinary individuals is astounding and should be noted. The examples of the young and old, male and female, exhibiting extreme empathy and compassion for a fellow human being is endless. Some examples include:

On May 11, 2013 a group of teenagers headed to prom in a stretch limo when a van near them skidded out of control and slammed into the side barrier, flipping over. Adorned in tuxes and prom dresses, the kids and the limo driver pulled over to help. Working together, despite the blood and jagged metal which stained and tore their prom attire, the limo driver and teenagers freed the trapped passengers, including a little boy who was smashed under the seat.

In Denver Colorado, Mary Bussey and her son, were on a walk when she noticed something dangling from a third floor balcony. She raced over when she realized it was a small child. She stood under the child and waited for him to fall, gently catching him without injury to the child.

In Michigan, James Patterson, fourteen years old, was babysitting his two younger siblings when he heard frantic banging and a woman screaming for help on his door step. He opened the door to a woman wrapped in clear packing tape with a bruised and bloodied face. She said she'd been sexually assaulted and held at gunpoint but was able to jump from his car. James let her in the house quickly and locked all of the doors. He grabbed his hunting knife and directed everyone to the bathroom where he locked them in. As he was calling 911, he heard the perpetrator, Eric Ramsey, pounding on the door, yelling; "I'm going to kill you!" When Ramsey couldn't break in, he began dousing gasoline on the house and set it on fire. Thankfully, help arrived and put out the blaze. The perpetrator escaped, but was later shot and killed.

In Pennsylvania, Temar Boggs and his friend Chris, recognized a young girl in the front seat of a car who fit the description of a missing person they had seen on the news. They chased after the car on their bicycles. When the kidnapper realized he was recognized and was being chased, he let the girl out at the next stoplight.

In 2011, Kole Devisscher noticed a blue jacket floating in the freezing waters of the river. Perplexed, he pulled over to get a better look and realized it was a young boy trapped in the ice. He quickly harnessed a tow strap to his truck and attempted to pull the boy out of the water. The boy was unable able to grip the rope because his hands were frozen, so Devisscher created a loop in the rope and lassoed the boy around the chest, pulling him to safety.

On May 8, in the parking lot of Sacramento Valley High School, a mom was picking up her daughter when she hit the car in front of her. Stunned, she put the car in reverse, not realizing her daughter was behind the car. She hit her daughter who became trapped underneath the vehicle. The baseball team was practicing nearby and heard the mom's blood curdling screams. They leaped over the practice fences to help. Surrounding the car, they lifted it off the ground so their coach could pull the young lady out safely.

Jamal Harris and Aaron Arias noticed a woman in the back seat of the car ahead of them at a stop sign. She looked terrified when she turned around. She touched the back of the windshield and mouthed, "Help me." The young men new she was in trouble and pursued the car. They called 911 and stayed with car, swerving in and out of traffic until the police apprehended the perpetrator.

During a mass shooting at Virginia Tech, Liviu Librecu, a professor and a Holocaust survivor, used his own body to barricade the door or his classroom, allowing most of his students' time to escape out the window. Liviu died after multiple shots rang through the door into his body.

There are countless stories of ordinary men and women who compassionately risk their lives to help complete strangers. Yet, our day to day relationships seem to be comprised of the opposite. The emotional destruction of human beings through humiliation and degradation seem to be more prevalent than ever. Even more disheartening is the fact that it involves people we are supposed to cherish and protect: wives, husbands, classmates, friends, co-workers, clients, etc. Why? Why do we hate when we are capable of love? How do groups of people decompensate into heartless individuals who are incapable of empathy for another human being?

The answer is projective identification. Projective identification only occurs when people exist amongst each other. In a marriage, a classroom, a social circle, professional space, etc. In addition, projective identification only exists if there are projectors. Projectors raise projectors, so we can only stop the cycle by stopping the projectors. It may be impossible for projectors to stop bullying and abusing others, but it is not impossible for the non-projectors in the world to avoid joining in. Ideally, if non-projectors stand up to the projectors politely but assertively, they have extreme power in helping to end the dynamic. If that doesn't work, remember, outsmart them! Inside, we are more powerful than the hate someone projects onto us, and because of this, we can always win by pulling ahead in life anyway your strengths, gifts, and talents allow.

Chapter 19

TERRORISM PERPETUATED

Acts of Terrorism such as school shootings, bombings, airplane hijackings, and hostage situations are horrifically frightening for victims. Research conducted about the effects of these experiences on the survivors, shows that trauma especially prolonged trauma, changes the brain. Victims are in a state of hyper-arousal during the trauma, psychologically, emotionally, and physically, their brain cannot process the experience like it would a normal memory. The experience is fragmented. Emotions are separated from the victim's sensory experiences, such as; what they saw, heard and smelled. The memory is fragmented, and cannot be filed away like other memories. The bits and pieces of recollection float around in the brain, ready to break to the surface and flood the victim with panic. Sometimes, it is the remnants of the victim's sensory experience that trigger the onslaught of terrifying emotions. These attacks can happen at any time and are often referred to as flashbacks or panic attacks. Not only can un-stored emotions come flooding back to wreak havoc, but thoughts may as well. Intrusive and intense thoughts connected with the experience, can overwhelm the victim and paralyze them in a state of terror.

Flashbacks, nightmares, disturbing thoughts, and panic attacks are all symptoms of PTSD, or *Post Traumatic Stress Disorder*. The most severe symptom of PTSD is called, disassociation. Disassociation is a defense mechanism used by everyone, and in small doses it can be healthy. A daydream or an episode of "spacing out," is an adaptive way for people to escape the monotony of daily life for a moment. In traumatic situations, however, the need for extreme disassociation can be defensive short term, but problematic in the long run. For example, if a crazed lunatic is holding a gun to a victim's temple, the victim is going to have to do something psychologically to tolerate the interaction without going absolutely crazy. The victim goes somewhere else, psychologically. Perhaps they stare at a spot on the wall and think about how it got there. Many, find themselves floating above their body, looking at themselves from above. Whatever the victim has to do, psychologically, to escape the traumatic situation for a moment in order to maintain themselves, they will and should do. Although it is protective in nature during the event, disassociation can cause prolonged problems for the victims neurologically. Disassociation stops the victim from remembering the traumatic event cohesively. Without a consolidated and organized memory, equipped with the emotions they were feeling at the time, the traumatic event will not be stored and eventually forgotten. Then it will rise, and overtake the victim any chance it gets. Furthermore, disassociation can block conscious awareness in some individuals, which allows them to operate without feeling or responsibility.

When the terror and panic of the traumatic incident continues to rush to the surface, even months after the incident, the victims suffer and react in several different ways.

1. They surrender to it, and become massively depressed and paralyzed.

2. They identify with the aggressor and become violent.

3. They escape through the use of drugs and alcohol.

4. They get professional help.

The critical thing to consider after episodes of violence is whether the victim is a projector themselves. If a projector is the victim in a terrorist attack or traumatic incident, chances are strong that they will become increasingly abusive and dangerous. A projector is already extremely emotionally fragile, which fuels their need to project. Adding the terror of a trauma will certainly come close to destroying what little self-esteem they have. A projector gains security and safety by dismantling someone else, thus they will need to do so tenfold after a trauma. If they feel constantly threatened, whether real or imagined, they feel entitled to destroy anyone, in any way they can. Already prone to rage, a projector's rage will intensify and become uncontrollable.

Twenty-four school shootings occurred following the twelve months since the Sandy Hook massacre. In all of these incidents, the shooters motivation was retribution of some kind. They felt victimized by something in their past and wanted revenge. Some shooters had been sexually abused, some had been unable to sustain relationships with their peers and experienced this as rejection and as an attack, and some were bullied. Nonetheless, these shooters had one thing in common, they all externalized blame, and wanted to hurt people to get revenge.

The three worst school shootings in the history of this country, Columbine, Virginia Tech, and Sandy Hook are examples of this. Each of the shooters involved had personality disorders, and were projectors. All had spent several years functioning on the outskirts of social life. The shooters had been unable to sustain positive relationships with their classmates and peers, and interpreted this as mass rejection on the most personal level. They felt victimized, and as victims they felt entitled to attack back. This allowed them to feel brave and powerful rather than weak and rejected. As distorted as it is, they felt like their own hero. If projectors are victims of terrorism, chances are they will terrorize, not only in their own homes but into the world perpetuating violence and trauma. Repeating and reproducing hate and destruction every opportunity they have, violence creates violence, when a projector is involved.

Recipients have a different response. Prone to guilt and the tendency to overly take responsibility for situations, recipients will suffer from profound survival guilt. Depression, anxiety, and shame will consume them for a long time. Hopefully, because they are self-reflective and self-aware, they will seek professional help. In time, they will grieve what was lost, and find a way to fight for the victims who lost their lives. They will likely spend their days championing this cause, attempting to end violence instead of perpetuating it. A much healthier, humane, and evolved response, which helps to stop the cycle of violence rather than spreading it.

Following some of the parents who lost their children at Sandy Hook, we see marvelous examples of people who have mustered up the strength to turn suffering into advocacy. It is tragic to even imagine an innocent, beautiful child terrorized and shot to death by an adult human being. How these parents go on living in a society where an innocent child is taken violently and intentionally from them is a miracle. Yet, they do. They do not attack back, instead several have created charities that help families with young children. One entitled, "Dillon's Wings for Change," supports children with autism. These parents, who have endured the most painful loss a human being can experience, have replaced their vengeful desires with the aspiration to help others. They choose to love instead of hate. Help instead of destroy. Create joy instead of pain, while finding peace instead of inflicting terror.

Chapter 20

HUMANNESS

When individuals operate from a hierarchal stance, with the belief that some human beings are more important than others, they are operating from a pathological position which breeds violence. No human being has the right to humiliate, condemn, bully, or ostracize another. The amount of money a human being makes, the number of degrees someone has, the social circle a person belongs to, the church that one is a part of, the number of years someone has been married, etc., does not make them more important than someone else.

The value we have for human life should be universal. People contribute to society in different ways and with different sets of gifts and talents. Our society is filled with numbers which give value to a humans, such as amount of money someone makes, their GPA, their class rank, their number of degrees, and number of cars they own. These numbers symbolize and represent a value that does not include the content of their character. It doesn't account for their ability to have compassion for fellow human beings, their desire to treat others with kindness, their ability to care for the downtrodden and hurt, or their drive to nurture and love children selflessly and with an open heart. If there was a number or ranking for kindness, tolerance, empathy, and the drive to keep peace in this world alive, we would be on a far more progressive path as a society.

The number of school shootings is rising substantially. The amount of children tortured and emotionally mistreated at school by their peers is astronomical. The percentage of young men and women who take their lives, or cut and mutilate their bodies as a way to cope with the emotional violence they face is mind boggling. If we want to keep our children safe, we must value character instead of hierarchy. Projectors must be corrected so that violence may come to an end. We must all look inside ourselves for the strength and ability to stand up for what is right. Just as projectors and bullies have proved that there is strength in numbers, good people can prove the same thing when rallying together to promote kindness and love.

A character logical disorder in which the individual displays a pervasive pattern of disregard for the rights of others; having tendencies to exploit and manipulate others. They often violate the law and lack a conscious.

Feelings of intense worry and stress.

A mental disorder in which the individual afflicted has erratic mood swings, difficulty managing their anger, impulsivity, and unstable relationships with others. The disorder is characterized by the individuals with lack of incite, inability to take responsibility for themselves in their interpersonal relationships, a tendency to play the victim, frequent rage, and lack of empathy.

An individual who imposes domination of another; repeatedly and habitually. Often using humiliation and degradation as tactics.

The force of getting one party to involuntarily act using threats and intimidation. To treat someone with disgust and disrespect.

To strip an individual of their human qualities, deeming them an animal or object.

Defense mechanisms are one way of looking at how people distance themselves from full awareness of unpleasant thoughts, feelings and behaviors.

Characterized by an individual's pervasive dependence on others to fulfill their responsibilities, needs and wishes. Similar to all personality disorders the individual lacks insight, empathy, and an awareness of other people's feelings because they are preoccupied with their own. They often have erratic mood swings, depressive episodes, and bouts of rage.

A pervasive pattern of sadness, low mood, lethargy, fatigue and lack of motivation and hopelessness.

Reduce or underestimate the worth or value of. Used in splitting. Attributing exaggeratedly negative qualities to the self or others.

: The evolving and maturing of a human being.

To deprive someone else of power or worth.

A temporary detachment from reality, while maintaining aware of reality.

To rule over or control.

The application of different sets of principles to two different people or populations.

The self. Identity. Sense of self. The part of the self that is most consciously aware.

The capacity to recognize emotions that are being experienced by others.

An involuntary reoccurring memory. A sudden re-experiencing of a terrifying experience.

A pervasive pattern of reacting in an emotional and dramatic manner in order to draw attention to oneself. Also characterized by a lack of empathy, insight, and ability to take responsibility for themselves in relationships. Often an individual with histrionic personality disorder plays the victim in order to gain attention and sympathy.

Identification is a psychological process whereby the subject assimilates an aspect, property, or attribute of the other and is transformed, wholly or partially, by the model the other provides.

Inpsychoanalytic theory, when an individual is unable to integrate difficult feelings, specific defenses are mobilized to overcome what the individual perceives as an unbearable situation. The defense that helps in this process is called splitting. Splitting is the tendency to view events or people as either all bad or all good.[1] When viewing people as all good, the individual is said to be using the defense mechanism idealization: a mental mechanism in which the person attributes exaggeratedly positive qualities to the self or others.

Unconsciously taking on someone else's attributes, feelings or beliefs and making them your own.

the process of one person replicating in herself/himself the behaviors, attributes and feelings of another.

When a person is plagued with self-doubt and uncertainty; unconfident and anxious.

To influence someone unscrupulously and subversively.

Extreme egocentrism, vanity and grandiosity.

A condition in which people have an excessive sense of self-importance, an extreme preoccupation with themselves, and lack of empathy for others. They lack the ability for insight and are unable to take responsibility for their actions in interpersonal relationships. They often feign the victim and externalize blame.

The state of being unbiased and not influenced by emotions or personal prejudices.

Becoming overwhelmed and physically incapacitated by extreme panic and anxiety.

To continue on and repeat.

A type of mental disorder in which you have a rigid and unhealthy pattern of thinking, functioning and behaving, characterized by a lack of insight into interpersonal relations, a tendency to externalize blame instead of taking responsibility, a heightened sense of self importance, a lack of empathy for others, and a tendency to believe they are the victims in almost every situation.

The experience of being projected on which brings about overwhelming feelings of self-doubt and worthlessness, in addition to extreme anxiety and sadness.

To further.

Posttraumatic stress disorder is an anxiety disorder in which an individual's ability to function is impaired by emotional responses to memories of a traumatic event. It's characterized by experiences of extreme panic, flashbacks, nightmares, a state of hyper vigilance, and bouts of depression. A person unconsciously rejects his or her own unacceptable attributes by ascribing them to someone else.

Projective identification is a term introduced by Melanie Klein to describe the process whereby in a close relationship, as between mother and child, lovers, or therapist and patient, hated parts of the self may be transferred unconsciously and forced into the other person.

An individual who is vulnerable to taking in the unconscious parts of someone else. Often, this leads to an increased capacity for empathy

: Vengeance. Revenge.

Your sense of self and your sense of self confidence.

The feelings and beliefs one has about themselves.

A defense mechanism caused by a failure in a person's thinking to bring together both positive and negative qualities of the self and others into a cohesive, realistic whole. The splitting defense allows a person to think in extremes i.e. an individual's actions or motivations are all good or all bad with no in between.

To obey someone without question. To be submissive, subdued, passive, and compliant with another's wishes. The use of violence and intimidation in the pursuit of political or emotional aims.

An emotional, physiological, neurological, and psychological response to a sudden and terrifying life event.

The part of the mind occurs automatically and is not available to introspection, and includes thought processes, memory, affect and motivation. Even though these processes exist well under the surface of conscious awareness, they often dictate a person's behaviors.

The content of the mind that an individual is not aware of.

The unconscious placement of ones feelings of self-loathing onto another in order to feel better about themselves.

React emotionally often with anger.

Made in the
USA
Middletown, DE

76340203R00070